Preparing to Receive Jesus

A Hands-On Religion Resource

Catholic Heritage Curricula

1-800-490-7713   *www.chcweb.com*

Credits:

Image credits: **pgs. i, vi, v, 4-top**: © Anne Simoneau; **pg. 20**: © Andre Adams / Shutterstock; **pg. 24**: © SavaSylan / Shutterstock; **pg. 27**: © LekaBo / Shutterstock; **pgs. 29, 32**: © Anne Simoneau; **pg. 33**: © CHC; **pgs. 36, 38-left, 43-right, 44-left**: © Renata Sedmakova / Shutterstock; **pg. 44-right**: © DenisFilm / Shutterstock; **pg. 49-right**: © Zvonimir Atletic / Shutterstock; **pg. 50-left**: © Zvonimir Atletic / Shutterstock; **pg. 50-right**: "Parvulus Pastor" by Mother Mary Nealis. © United States - Canada Province of the Society of the Sacred Heart; **pg. 51-left**: © Renata Sedmakova / Shutterstock; **pg. 51-right**: © Claudia Paulussen / Shutterstock; **pg. 66**: © Anne Simoneau; **pg. 67**: © Libe Makarova / Shutterstock

Cover image: © Anne Simoneau

Grateful acknowledgment is made for permission to use excerpts from *The Faith Explained, Third Edition* by Leo J. Trese. Copyright © 1965 by Fides/Claretian. By permission of Scepter Publishers, New Rochelle, NY.

ISBN: 978-1-946207-00-5

Printed by Bookmasters
Ashland, OH
February 2018

Catholic Heritage Curricula
1-800-490-7713 www.chcweb.com

"*Oh, that I might lodge in Your tent forever,
take refuge in the shelter of Your wings!*"

—*Psalm 61:5*

BOOK
Table of Contents

PACKET *(sold separately)*
Table of Contents

Preparing to Receive Jesus

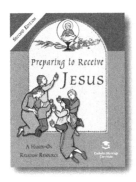

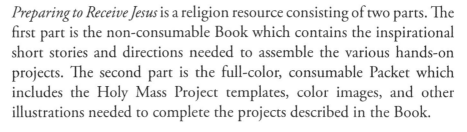

Preparing to Receive Jesus is a religion resource consisting of two parts. The first part is the non-consumable Book which contains the inspirational short stories and directions needed to assemble the various hands-on projects. The second part is the full-color, consumable Packet which includes the Holy Mass Project templates, color images, and other illustrations needed to complete the projects described in the Book.

Preparing to Receive Jesus includes many stories and hands-on activities to help "bring to heart" the lessons your child is learning in his catechism. It is not meant to replace your child's catechism lessons but to enrich them. As a supplement to the catechism, this twenty-one-week course provides an excellent preparation for receiving the sacraments of Reconciliation and First Holy Communion. Lessons are designed to be completed at a rate of one per week, but can be accelerated to several lessons per week if need be. Spend as much one-on-one time as possible as you read the stories and work together with your child on the projects, allowing ample time for questions and discussion.

A family or group using *Preparing to Receive Jesus* will need to purchase only one Book, while each student using the course will need his own Packet. If you are using this course with more than one child, additional Packets may be purchased from Catholic Heritage Curricula at *www.chcweb.com*.

The Faith Explained (Third Edition) by Fr. Leo J. Trese is a highly recommended parent resource. The suggested readings listed throughout the course are short and very helpful. They not only provide a timely review, but give the parent the necessary background information needed to teach the subject matter naturally.

Additional enrichment resources for your home library:

> *My Little Missal*
> *The Weight of a Mass*
> *Little Catechism on the Eucharist*
> *Traditional Catholic Hymns: Hymns of Praise* CD

For older children receiving the sacraments for the first time:

> *The King of the Golden City*

Catholic Heritage Curricula

1-800-490-7713   *www.chcweb.com*

Introduction

The Essentials

"Neither for First Confession nor for First Communion is full and perfect knowledge of Christian doctrine requisite. But the child ought afterwards gradually to learn the entire catechism according to his capacity."
—*Pope St. Pius X*

As you prepare your child for his first reception of the Sacraments, keep in mind his maturity level. Learning the truths of our Faith is a gradual process. The subject matter is very abstract in nature. First impressions of the truths of our Faith will be hazy at first, and will need to be renewed and strengthened by repetition, experience, and time.

The Essence

"The spirit of the catechetical apostolate is not the catechism for its own sake, but the catechism lived and presented as a model of life."

In *Preparing to Receive Jesus*, simple truths are presented in a variety of interesting ways, allowing your child to more easily receive and understand the material, as opposed to an overabundance of dry material which is difficult to digest and assimilate. The illustrated examples in story format, together with the hands-on activities, are indispensable because their very concreteness can be easily grasped and understood, thus arousing a child's interest and inviting discussion. Once a child is receptive and begins to share and discuss, the rest will follow!

To be content with the mere recitation of a formula is to be satisfied with teaching the catechism for its own sake. Our primary goal is to encourage and motivate our children to do what our Holy Faith teaches. Undoubtedly, then, our chief concern as parents is to instill in the hearts of our children a true and personal love for Jesus.

Remember the familiar adage that "the Faith is caught, not taught." With a young child, it is as much our manner and example as the materials we use that will make the biggest impression. Our expression, smile, tone of voice, manner of speaking (animated or otherwise), the way we live and act—these are what draw a child to love God. As Sir Arnold Lunn said, "One fire kindles another!"

Part One: Reconciliation

Overview of Lessons 1–7

**"This is the definition of sin:
the misuse of powers given by God for doing good,
a use contrary to God's commandments." —St. Basil**

PREPARATION

Excerpts from *The Faith Explained* by Fr. Leo Trese, chapters 29, 30, and 31, are included in each lesson. It is highly recommended that the parent reads the entire chapters in order to teach these important concepts.

Encouraging your child to cultivate a forgiving attitude is an important focus as your child learns more about God's mercy in the Sacrament of Reconciliation. Remind your child how we often ask God in the "Our Father" prayer to forgive us our sins **as** we forgive those who hurt us. Encourage your child to show prompt and sincere forgiveness by teaching him to respond with "I forgive you" after receiving a verbal apology from someone who has hurt him.

 **PACKET**

PAGES 1–4

Welcome Letter

Color and fill in the Welcome Letter, then cut it out and mail it to your child. While your letter is in the mail, work together with your child on the Words to Know on pages 3–4 of the Packet. See answers below.

mercy – a willingness to forgive

forgive – to stop being angry with someone who has hurt me

offend – to do wrong to someone

sacrifice – giving up something; an offering to God

sorrow – sadness

penance – a prayer or action that "makes up" for sin

sacrament – an outward sign (using common things in my life) instituted by Christ (chosen by Jesus) to give grace (that give me a share in God's life)

confess – to tell someone what I've done wrong

conscience – an inner "knowing" when an action is wrong

temptation – a strong desire for something that would not be good for me

Reconciliation – the sacrament where I meet Jesus and He forgives my sins

absolve – the priestly action of forgiving my sins

Part One: Reconciliation expands upon the five steps of making a good confession, with stories to illustrate each key point. This section concludes with a gentle examen and hands-on preparation for receiving the Sacrament of Penance.

Lesson 1: Introduction to Confession

📖 Book: pages 4–6
    Activity: Pepper and Water Demonstration
    Story: "Jeff"

✂ Packet: pages 5–6
    Project: Act of Contrition Prayer Card

Lesson 2: Examination of Conscience

📖 Book: pages 7–10
    Story: "Apples, Ripe and Rosy, Sir"

✂ Packet: pages 7–10
    Project: Child's Examen

Lesson 3: Sorrow for Sin

📖 Book: pages 11–16
    Story: "That Red Silk Frock"

✂ Packet: pages 11–16
    Project: That Red Silk Frock

Lesson 4: Purpose of Amendment

📖 Book: pages 17–20
    Story: "Suzy's Dragon"

✂ Packet: pages 17–20
    Project: St. Michael Prayer Card

Lesson 5: Confession of Sins

📖 Book: pages 21–24
    Story: "What a Dollar Bought"

✂ Packet: pages 21–22
    Project: Confession Card

Lesson 6: Penance

📖 Book: pages 25–28
    Activity: Confession Practice
    Story: "The Broken Flowerpot"

✂ Packet: pages 23–24
    Activity: Confession Bookmark

Lesson 7: Preparation for First Confession

📖 Book: pages 29–31
    Story: "Did You Say *Mortal* Sin?"

✂ Packet: pages 25–28
    Project: Simplified Ten Commandments
    Project: Showing My Love for God

Lesson 1: Introduction to Confession

To begin this section, read the parable of the Prodigal Son to your child (Luke 15:11–32). Briefly go through the parable and show how the Prodigal Son's process—from realizing he had sinned to confessing to his father—is similar to the steps we go through when we make a good confession.

I   He **thought** about what he had done wrong.
(examination of conscience)
O my God, I am heartily sorry for having offended You, . . .

II   He was **sorry** for what he had done.
(sorrow for our sins)
. . . I detest all my sins because of Your just punishments, but most of all because they offend You, my God, Who are all good and deserving of all my love . . .

III He **made up his mind to go back to his father**.
(firm purpose of amendment)
. . . I firmly resolve, with the help of Your grace, . . .

IV He **confessed** his sins.
(tell our sins to a priest)
. . . to confess my sins, . . .

V   He was **ready to do anything his father said**.
(do the penance the priest gives us)
. . . to do penance, and to amend my life.

The Prodigal Son

When we do wrong (lie, disobey) or hurt others (talk meanly, hit or shove) we know it. Our conscience lets us know when we have done wrong. We feel unhappy with ourselves. We can either obey the urgings of our conscience to repent or we can pretend it does not bother us.

Here is another illustration showing the process of repentance, and of acting on the promptings of our conscience. A boy named John loved his mother deeply, but one day he disobeyed her many times. This is what he did that evening:

1. Thought of the ways he had hurt his mother that day.
2. "Owned up" to what he had done wrong.
3. Told his mother he was truly sorry.
4. Promised to be more obedient.
5. Dried the dishes cheerfully to make up for the wrong he had done.

 STORY   Read aloud "Jeff" on page 6 of the Book as an illustration of sin, its consequences, and the wonderful gift of the Sacrament of Penance.

 **PACKET**
PAGE 5

Have your child write out the Act of Contrition on the lines provided on the Prayer Card. When your child has written the Act of Contrition, cut out the front and back of the card, glue them back to back on colorful cardstock, and laminate for durability. Invite your child to use the Prayer Card each evening before bed to begin memorizing the Act of Contrition. Having the prayer memorized lessens anxiety when going to confession.

One way to introduce a short examen at the end of the day is to invite your child to think: "Can I offer this whole day to God as a gift of love?" An Act of Contrition asks forgiveness for any sins of the day and strengthens our resolve for tomorrow. It is not the form of examining that is important, but the heartfelt desire to please God.

ACTIVITY—PEPPER AND WATER DEMONSTRATION

Perform the following demonstration with your child to illustrate the meaning of purity.

Introduction: "The Sacrament of Reconciliation keeps our souls pure. When something is pure we mean that it is completely and truly what it is and not mixed with anything else. Picture pure white snow as it falls from the sky and piles up in drifts, or a flawless diamond sparkling brilliantly in the light. We are pure too, when we are not 'mixed up' with sin. (Who was the purest human being that God created? Yes, the Blessed Virgin Mary! We call her 'Mother, Most Pure.')"

Preparation: Make a cross with a grease pencil or place a cross sticker on the inside base of a clear glass bowl. "The cross represents God's will—how He wants us to live so we can be happy."

Demonstration: Pour clean, clear water into the glass bowl. "Can you see the cross through the water? Yes, when we are pure we can see God's will for our lives."

Now add a tablespoon of pepper to the water. "The pepper is like sin which clouds our vision of God. It is hard to see the cross (God's will) through the dirty water. The impurities in the water make the water less than what it is, just like sin makes us impure and less able to know and do God's will."

Dip a toothpick into dish soap and then touch the toothpick to the top of the peppered water. "See how the pepper scatters! The Sacrament of Confession acts even more immediately and completely in removing sin from our souls, returning our souls to a state of purity and making us true children of God—what God made us to be."

STORY   THE SILVER LOCKETS

Once there were two little girls named Mary and Lucy. Their father gave each of them a silver locket and inside of each locket was a costly pearl. Their father told the girls that they must take good care of the lockets on account of the pearls. He told them that when they were older they could open the lockets and see the pearls. After a while Lucy grew tired of taking care of her locket. She began to think that the pearl might not be worth very much anyway and one day she threw it aside thoughtlessly. But Mary knew that her father meant every word he had said, and year after year she guarded her locket with the greatest care. At last she was old enough and all the family stood about her as her father unfastened the locket. Lo! there was a pearl of the purest white, so beautiful that for a moment they all held their breath! Then Lucy thought of her locket and she ran to look for it but it was lost. God is our Father and He has given each of us a priceless pearl in a silver locket. The locket is our body and the pearl is our soul. He wants us to take care of our soul so we can be happy with Him forever in Heaven.

Jeff

A little boy named Jeff was very fond of horses. His greatest delight was to go to the stable and feed and pet them. Now one of the horses, the black one, Raven, was not a safe animal to pet. He could not be trusted. When he seemed most friendly, he would suddenly turn around and bite, or strike out with his hoofs. So Jeff had been told to give up patting and petting this dangerous play-fellow and to keep out of the stable. Jeff's father, a doctor, knew what a terrible thing a kick might be, and it was because he loved his little son dearly that he forbade him to do what would hurt him.

Did the boy do as he was told? No. After a time he began to peep into the stable; then he went just inside; and at last, when no one was looking, he would go in and play with the horse as before. "I wonder why father forbade me," he said. "Raven has never kicked me yet and he never will. I am not afraid. I will not go too near. No harm will come."

One afternoon the doctor left home to visit a sick woman who lived just across the way. He had not been in her house more than five minutes when his oldest son, all out of breath, came in. "Oh, Father, come home at once. Jeff has been in the stable and Raven has kicked him. He is lying in Mother's arms unconscious." The father hurried home and into the yard. There by the stable door was a little sad crowd—brothers and sisters, around the boy who lay in his mother's lap, his face and hair covered with blood that kept trickling from a deep gash in the forehead. His father carried him upstairs and laid him on his bed. When the father came out of the room, he looked very grave.

"The boy's head is badly hurt," he said, "and he must be kept very quiet. I shall send for a nurse." The brothers looked sad and the sisters began to cry.

"Will he get better, Father?" they asked.

"Yes, if he takes my medicine and does just as I tell him. I will put some ointment on the cuts and bruises to take away the pain and make them heal."

For many days Jeff lay in bed all in the dark. No one, I think, would have known him, except perhaps his mother, his face was so swollen and ugly, black and blue with bruises. He saw the sunshine trying to come in through the blinds.

He heard his brothers and sisters in the garden laughing and shouting at their play, and he wondered if he would ever be in the garden and play in the sunshine again. But he had learned a good lesson. He did as he was told now. And whenever his father brought the ointment, he let him put it on without a word.

Poor little Jeff! He did so want to be well again. And he did get well. One by one the ugly marks the black horse had made went away, and his little face looked as it had been before. It was a good thing for him that his father had the medicine and precious ointment ready. Without that he might have died.

Now let us think of another Father, another sick child, and another injury a great deal worse than Jeff's. The good Father Who forbids His child to do what would hurt him is God, the Divine Physician. The injury that comes of disobedience is sin. The child who hurts himself by disobeying his Father is me. But what is it that will make me well again? God gives us the Divine Remedy in the Sacrament of Penance!

Jeff's father was very kind. He did not scold his little injured child, but brought him something to cure him. So does our Heavenly Father. He has a precious cure ready for our sore souls—oh, how precious it is! It is the Precious Blood of His Son, Jesus. When we confess our sins in the Sacrament of Penance, we receive the cure of God's forgiveness.

—Adapted from a story written in 1902

Lesson 2: Examination of Conscience

PREPARATION   To prepare for this lesson please read pages 439–442 in *The Faith Explained*.

"The question is, is our examination of conscience as thorough and as earnest as it might be? It is easy, particularly if we receive the sacrament of Penance often, to grow quite casual about this examination of conscience. 'It's about the same as last time,' we say to ourselves. 'Missed my morning prayers, used God's name irreverently a couple of times, got angry maybe once, told two or three lies.' With that quick roundup, we hold ourselves ready for confession. We seem to forget that it is a *sacrament* which we are about to receive, a sacrament for whose efficacy Christ died in agony. Our examination of conscience ought to be an unhurried and careful preparation; otherwise, it will be no wonder if our quota of grace is small."

The Faith Explained by Fr. Leo Trese, pg. 440. Reprinted with permission, courtesy of Scepter Publishers, New Rochelle, NY.

THEME   **I   He thought about what he had done wrong.**
(examination of conscience)

O my God, I am heartily sorry for having offended You. I detest all my sins because of Your just punishments, but most of all because they offend You, my God, Who are all good and deserving of all my love. I firmly resolve, with the help of Your grace, to confess my sins, to do penance, and to amend my life. Amen.

 STORY   Read aloud "Apples, Ripe and Rosy, Sir" on the following pages to illustrate the importance of making an examination of conscience.

EXAMEN   Discuss the different points in the story. Was it wrong for Tom to take the money from the mantel without asking? How did Widow Barry help Tom to examine his conscience? Like Tom, we need to examine our conscience—think of our sins—so we can be truly sorry for all that does not please God. *We want to know our failings so that we can improve.*

One question we can ask ourselves when we aren't sure if something is wrong is, "Would I want my parents, friends, siblings to know what I plan to do/say/act?" We can pretty much bet that if we don't want to talk to someone about it, or we hide it, we should not do it.

 PACKET

PAGES 7–10

Cut out each section of the Child's Examen along the dotted lines as indicated. Put them into an envelope and begin studying and discussing one section every few days. Talk about why the action is sinful[1] and why it offends God,[2] hurts our relationship with others, and hurts us. Emphasize how God's laws are like the gentle, loving arms of Jesus wrapped tenderly around us for our own protection. No one loves us or wants our salvation more than God!

When your child has finished all the sections, have him "order" them in a way that is most helpful to him. For example, if he has trouble obeying, encourage him to put this section on top. Sections may be glued onto a piece of colored cardstock or kept in the envelope.

---

[1] Sin is choosing to do wrong; to disobey God.

[2] Sin offends God because it is rebellion of a creature against God, its creator, because it denies God the honor which is due to Him. "Offend" comes from Latin words which mean "to strike against." To offend God means to refuse to give God the love He deserves. Fr. Leo Trese explains, "A sin is a refusal to give God our obedience, a refusal to give God our love. Since every bit of us belongs to God, and the whole purpose of our existence is to love God, it follows that every bit of us owes obedience to God."

Apples, Ripe and Rosy, Sir

The temperature was sharp and frosty, the ground white, the clouds heavy with snow. The storm of the night before had only ceased temporarily; it would begin again soon—a few flakes were already floating in the air. By early afternoon the children began to troop out of their homes. How pleasant to watch the throng of bright-eyed, chattering little girls, in coats and hoods and mittens, and a crowd of sturdy boys trudging along discussing games and sports, and others indulging in a little random snowballing of their comrades. Half an hour later the snow was falling thick and fast. A number of boys had gathered in one of the parks and were busy completing a snowfort. People hurried home; it was sure to be a disagreeable evening.

These indications were sadly noted by one person in particular, to whom they meant more than to others in general. This was the good, old Irishwoman who kept the apple and peanut stand at the street corner, and who was the center of attraction to the children.

"Wisha, this is goin' to be a cold night, I'm thinkin'!" sighed she, wrapping a faded and much-worn shawl more securely about her, and striving to protect both herself and her wares beneath the shelter of an old umbrella. "What bad luck I've had today!" she continued under her breath, still scanning the faces of the passersby, though she now had little hope that any would pause to buy. "An' it's a bigger lot than usual I laid in, too. The peanuts is extry size; an' them apples look so fine and rosy, I thought it 'ud make anybody's mouth water to see them. I counted upon the boys to buy them up in a twinklin', by reason of me markin' them down to two for a cent. An' so they would, but they're so taken up with sportin' in the snow that they can think of nothin' else. An' now that it's turned so raw, sure I'm afraid it's cold comfort any one but a lad would think it, settin' his teeth on edge tryin' to eat them. I'll tarry a bit longer; an' then I'll take meself to me little room, even though I'll have to drink me tea without a tint of milk or a dust of sugar tonight."

Patiently she waited. The clock struck five. As no other customers appeared, the old woman, who was known as Widow Barry, concluded that she would be movin' on home.

The stand consisted of a large basket, a campseat, and the umbrella, which was intended to afford, not only a roof, but an air of dignity to the stand, and was therefore always open, rain or shine.

To "shut up shop," though it meant simply to lower the umbrella, gather up the goods and depart, was to the apple vender a momentous affair. The widow was obliged literally to carry her establishment. To make her way, thus laden, in the midst of a driving snowstorm was indeed a difficult matter. Half a dozen times she faltered in discouragement. The street led over a steep hill; how was she to reach the top? She struggled along; the wind blew through her thin garments; the umbrella bobbed wildly about; her hands grew numb; the basket kept slipping from her grasp. Several persons passed, but no one seemed to think of stopping to assist her. A group of boys were sledding down the middle of the street; what did they care about the storm? Several boys, who were standing awaiting their turn, glanced idly at the poor woman.

With a laugh, Ed Brown sent a well-aimed snowball straight against the umbrella, which shook with a thud. Then the group whizzed by, without another thought of the aged creature toiling up the hill. No one appeared to have time to help her.

Presently, however, she heard a firm, light step behind her. The next moment a pair of merry brown eyes peered under the umbrella; a face beamed upon her with the smile of old friendship, and a happy, young voice cried out:

"Good afternoon, Mrs. Barry! It's hard work getting on today, isn't it?"

A gentle expression lighted up the apple-woman's weather-beaten face as she recognized the little fellow, who was evidently returning from an errand, as he carried a milk can in one hand while drawing a sled with the other.

"Indade an' it is, Tom!" she replied, pausing a second.

"Let us see if we can't manage differently," he went on, taking her burden and setting it upon the sled. "There, that is better."

"Oh, thank ye kindly! It's too much for ye to be takin' this trouble."

"No trouble at all," said he. "Follow me, I'll pick out the best places for you to walk in—the snow is drifting so!"

He trudged on ahead, glancing back occasionally to see if the basket and campseat were safe, or to direct her steps—as if all this were the most natural thing in the world for him to do, as in truth it was. He and Widow Barry had been good friends for some time. Tom, moreover, was a regular patron of "the stand."

"Sure, an' didn't he buy out me whole supply one day this last January?" she would say. "His birthday it was, and the dear boy was eleven years old. He spent the big silver dollar his grandfather gave him, a treatin' all the boys of the neighborhood to apples an' peanuts, an' sendin' me home to rest."

Upon reaching the Widow Barry's home, Tom scampered off with an especially good-looking apple, which the woman forced into his hand.

"Ah, but he's the dear, generous-hearted boy!" she exclaimed, as she stood looking after him. "There's not a bit of worldly pride or meanness about him. May the Lord keep him so! The only thing I'd be afraid of is that he'll be easily led. There's that Ed Brown now—Heaven forgive me, but somehow I don't like that lad. Though he's the son of the richest man in the neighborhood, he's no fit companion for Tom Norris, I'm thinkin'."

* * * *

As Widow Barry had thought, Tom was easily led, and therein rested the possibilities of great good or evil. As he mingled more with other boys, he was not always steadfast in acting up to his knowledge of what was right, and he was apt to be influenced by his companions. At present he was making a chum of Ed Brown, who, though only a year older, was shrewd and what the world calls "smart." Tom's mother had positively forbade Tom to have any more to do with Ed—a command which he grumbled a good deal about, and, alas, occasionally disobeyed.

But to continue our story. On the following Saturday morning, the skies were blue, the sun shone bright, the gladness of spring was in the air. The apple stand at the corner had a prosperous aspect. The umbrella, though shabbier than ever, had a cheery look. Widow Barry was engaged in polishing up her apples and arranging the peanuts as invitingly as possible; a number of pennies already jingled in the small bag attached to her apron string, in which she kept her money.

"Ah, here comes Tom!" she exclaimed, presently.

"Hello, Mrs. Barry!" cried he. "How's business today? Too early to tell yet? Well, see if I can't help it a little. Give me a dozen apples, and one—yes, two bags of nuts."

Pleased and flustered at this stroke of fortune, she busied herself in getting out two of the largest of her paper bags and filling the large order. But Tom was not like himself this morning. He had plenty to say; but he talked quickly with a kind of forced happiness, and he was eager to be off.

The old woman paused a second, as if suddenly impressed by the difference in his manner. With a pleasant word she put the well-filled bags into Tom's hands and received the money he offered in payment—three bright new dimes. At that moment she caught a glimpse of Ed Brown lurking by a house at the other end of the block. The sight filled her with a vague misgiving. She glanced at Tom.

"Wait a bit," she said, laying a hand upon his arm.

"What is the matter? Didn't I give you the right amount?" he asked impatiently.

The old woman bent forward and peered anxiously into his face; her kind but searching eyes seemed to look down into his very soul, as, in a voice trembling with emotion, she replied: "Yes. But tell me, where did ye get the money?"

Tom's face changed; he tried to put her off, saying, "Pshaw! Why do you want to ask a fellow such a question? Haven't I bought more than this from you before?"

"Ye have, dear; but not in this way, I'm thinkin'," she answered.

"It's all right. Do let me go, Mrs. Barry!" cried he, beginning to feel decidedly frightened.

"Hi, Tom, come on!" called Ed Brown, emerging from around the corner of the house.

"Look here, Tom, darlin'! You'll not move a step with them things, until I know where the money came from."

"Well, then," said Tom, doggedly, seeing that escape was impossible, "I got it at home, off the mantel in the sitting room."

"Oh, no!" exclaimed Mrs. Barry, raising her eyes toward Heaven, as if praying for the pardon of the offence.

"Why, that's nothing!" he went on. "Ed Brown says lots of boys do it. Some take the change out of their father's pockets even, if they get a chance. His father doesn't mind a bit. He always has plenty of cash, Ed has."

"Ah, yes, that ne'er-do-well, Ed Brown!" said the old woman, shaking her fist at the distant Ed, who, realizing that Tom had got into trouble, disappeared in a twinkling.

"An' his father don't mind! Then it's because he knows nothin' about it. They'll come a day of reckonin' for him. An' you—"

"Oh, my parents won't care!" persisted Tom, thoroughly ashamed, but still anxious to excuse himself. "Mother always says that everything in the house is for the use of the family. If we children should make a raid on the pantry, and carry off a pie or cake, she might punish us for the disobedience, but she wouldn't call it stealing." He blushed as he uttered the ugly word.

"Yes, but to take money is different, ye know,"

continued his relentless friend, whose heart was sorrowing over him with the tenderness of a mother for her child.

Tom was silent; he did know, had really known from the first, though now his fault stood before him in its ugliness; all the excuses with which he had attempted to hide it fell from it like a veil, showing the hateful thing it was. He could not bring himself to acknowledge it, however. Sullenly he set down the apples and peanuts, murmuring, "I never did it before, anyhow!"

"No, nor never will again, I'm sure, child! This'll be a lifelong lesson to ye," returned the old woman as she put the dimes back into his hand. "Go right home with them now, an' tell yer mother all about it."

"Tell my mother!" faltered Tom, doubtful of the consequences of such a confession.

"Yes. She'll be gentle with ye, never fear, if ye are really sorry."

"Indeed I am, Mrs. Barry," declared Tom, quite breaking down at last.

"I'm certain ye are, child!" continued the good woman, heartily. "An' when ye get home, go to yer own little room, an' there on yer bended knees ask God to forgive ye. Make up yer mind to shun bad friends for the future; an' never, from this hour, will we speak another word about this—save ye may come an' say: 'I've done as ye bid me, Mrs. Barry. It's all hunkey dory!'"

The old woman smiled with grim humor as she found herself quoting the boy's favorite slang expression.

Tom laughed in spite of himself, so funny did it sound from her lips; but at the same time he drew his jacket sleeve across his eyes, which had grown strangely dim, and said: "I will, Mrs. Barry. You may trust me: I will."

And Tom did. From that day he and the honest old applewoman were better friends than ever.

—Adapted from a story written in 1893

Lesson 3: Sorrow for Sin

PREPARATION   To prepare for this lesson, and to teach the difference between perfect and imperfect contrition, please read pages 442–444 in *The Faith Explained*.

"What then *is* this contrition that is so essential in order to receive the sacrament of Penance worthily? The word 'contrition' comes from a Latin word which means 'to grind, to pulverize.' The idea is that contrition reduces the self to dust, causes the self to stand before God in utter humility. The great Council of Trent, which gave exact wording to so much of Catholic doctrine, defined contrition as 'a sorrow of heart and hatred for sin committed, with the resolve to sin no more.'"

The Faith Explained by Fr. Leo Trese, pg. 442. Reprinted with permission, courtesy of Scepter Publishers, New Rochelle, NY.

THEME   **II**   He was **sorry** for what he had done.
                     (sorrow for our sins)

O my God, I am heartily sorry for having offended You. **I detest all my sins because of Your just punishments, but most of all because they offend You, my God, Who are all good and deserving of all my love.** I firmly resolve, with the help of Your grace, to confess my sins, to do penance, and to amend my life. Amen.

 STORY   Read aloud "That Red Silk Frock" on page 13 of the Book to encourage sorrow for sins.

EXAMEN   Discuss the different points in the story: Annie was first sorry because of what her friends would think (human respect) if they heard she had stolen the silk dress. This is an example of imperfect contrition. When Annie sank to the floor after looking at the picture of Jesus and Mary, the reason for her sorrow had changed. This is an example of perfect contrition. Do we care more about "looking good" to others or *being good* for love of God?

Why did Annie feel uncomfortable and turn the picture toward the wall? When we have something to hide, it is often because what we're doing is wrong. Discuss how Annie's "little" acts of disobedience led to stealing.

 PACKET

PAGES 11–16   Help your child complete the "That Red Silk Frock" activity by cutting out the words from the story and pasting them where they belong in the boxes provided. Answers may be found on the next page. When finished, the two pages may be glued to a larger piece of colored posterpaper and displayed. Discuss the different steps that led to Annie's contrition and repentance.

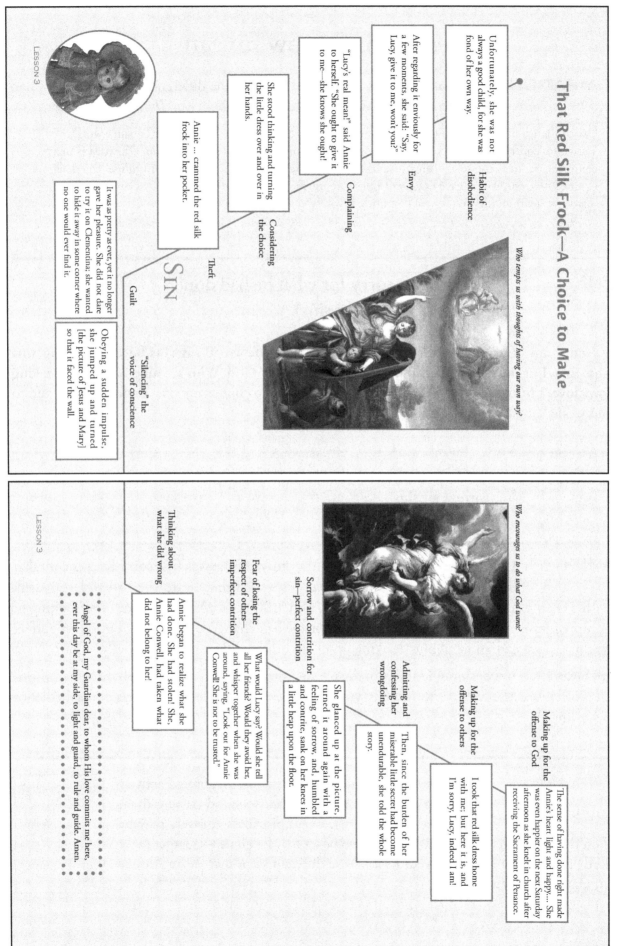

That Red Silk Frock—A Choice to Make

Who tempts us with thoughts of having our own way?

Unfortunately, she was not always a good child, for she was fond of her own way.
— Habit of disobedience

After regarding it enviously for a few moments, she said: "Say, Lucy, give it to me, won't you?"
— Envy

"Lucy's real mean!" said Annie to herself. "She ought to give it to me—she knows she ought!"
— Complaining

She stood thinking and turning the little dress over and over in her hands.
— Considering the choice

Annie ... crammed the red silk frock into her pocket.
— Theft

It was as pretty as ever, yet it no longer gave her pleasure. She did not dare to try it on Clementina; she wanted to hide it away in some corner where no one would ever find it.
— Guilt

Obeying a sudden impulse, she jumped up and turned [the picture of Jesus and Mary] so that it faced the wall.
— "Silencing" the voice of conscience

SIN

Who encourages us to do what God wants?

Annie began to realize what she had done. She had stolen! She, Annie Conwell, had taken what did not belong to her!
— Thinking about what she did wrong

What would Lucy say? Would she tell all her friends? Would they avoid her, and whisper together when she was around, saying: "Look out for Annie Conwell! She is not to be trusted."
— Fear of losing the respect of others—imperfect contrition

She glanced up at the picture, turned it around again with a feeling of sorrow, and, humbled and contrite, sank on her knees in a little heap upon the floor.
— Sorrow and contrition for sin—perfect contrition

Then, since the burden of her miserable little secret had become unendurable, she told the whole story.
— Admitting and confessing her wrongdoing

I took that red silk dress home with me; but here it is, and I'm sorry, Lucy, indeed I am!
— Making up for the offense to others

The sense of having done right made Annie's heart light and happy.... She was even happier on the next Saturday afternoon as she knelt in church after receiving the Sacrament of Penance.
— Making up for the offense to God

Angel of God, my Guardian dear, to whom His love commits me here, ever this day be at my side, to light and guard, to rule and guide. Amen.

That Red Silk Frock

You could not help but like little Annie Conwell; she was so full of fun. Unfortunately, she was not always a good child, for she was fond of her own way; and if she set her heart upon having anything, she wanted it without delay—right then and there.

Annie's great friend was Lucy Caryl. Lucy lived on the next block; and every day when out on an errand for her mother, Annie called for her, or Lucy ran down to play. Regularly Mrs. Conwell said: "Remember, Annie, I want you to come straight from errands, and not stop at the Caryls'. You may go and play with Lucy afterward, but you must come home first."

"Yes, 'um," was the quick answer Annie always made.

But, strange as it may seem, although Annie Conwell was considered clever, she seemed to have a wretched memory in regard to this rule, or else there were many good excuses for breaking the rule. When, as sometimes happened, she entered the house some two hours late, Mrs. Conwell reproachfully looked up from her sewing and asked: "What time is it, dear?"

And Annie, after a startled glance at the clock, either stammered, "O mother, I forgot!" or else rattled off an excuse.

"Very well!" was the frequent warning. "If you stay at Lucy Caryl's without permission, you must remain indoors on Saturday as a punishment for your disobedience."

Nevertheless, when the end of the week came, Annie usually managed to escape the threatened penalty. One special holiday, however, her mother surprised the little girl by saying, "Annie, I have told you over and over again that you must come directly home, and yet for several days you disobeyed me. I am going shopping now, and I forbid you to go out to play until I return."

Annie reddened and glanced at Mrs. Conwell's face. She silently walked to the window.

"It makes me so mad!" grumbled Annie, as she watched her mother leave. There was no use in standing idly thinking about it though, so Annie began to wonder what she should do. As she stood looking out the window, Annie saw Lucy Caryl who, from the opposite sidewalk, was making frantic efforts to attract her attention.

"Come into my house and play with me," Lucy spelled with her fingers in sign language.

Annie opened the window. "I can't, Lucy!" she called. "Mother said I must stay in the house."

"Oh, do come—just for a little while!" tempted naughty Lucy. "Your mother will never know. We'll watch the corner; when we see her coming, you can run around by the yard and slip in at the gate before she reaches the front door."

The temptation was strong. Annie pretended to herself that she did not understand the uneasy feeling in her heart, which told her she was doing wrong. She ran for her coat and in a few moments was running along the sidewalk with Lucy to the Caryls' spacious brownstone house.

"My Aunt Mollie sent me some lovely clothes for my doll," said Lucy. "The box is upstairs. Wait a minute while I run and get it."

When Lucy again joined her friend in their accustomed play corner, Lucy, with much satisfaction, displayed her present.

"Your Aunt Mollie must be so nice!" exclaimed Annie. "How lucky you are! Three more frocks for your doll! Clementina has not had any new clothes for a long time. I think that red silk dress is the prettiest, don't you?"

"I haven't quite decided," answered Lucy. "Christabel looks lovely in it; but I think the blue one is perhaps even more pretty."

They tried the various outfits on Lucy's doll, admiring the look of each in turn.

"Still, I like the red silk dress best," said Annie.

"It would just suit your doll, Clementina, wouldn't it?" suggested Lucy.

"Yes," sighed Annie, taking up the little frock, and imagining she saw her own doll attired in its gorgeousness. After regarding it enviously for a few moments, she said: "Say, Lucy, give it to me, won't you?"

"Why, the idea!" cried Lucy, aghast at the suggestion.

"I think you should," pouted Annie. "You hardly ever give me anything, although you are my dearest friend. I made you a present of Clementina's second best hat for Christabel, and only yesterday I gave you that ring you asked me for."

These unanswerable arguments were lost upon Lucy, however. She snatched away the tiny frock, and both little girls sulked a while.

"Lucy's real mean!" said Annie to herself. "She ought to give it to me—she knows she ought! Oh, dear, I want it awfully! She owes me something for what I've given her."

"I am going home," Annie announced aloud.

"Oh, no!" protested Lucy, aroused to the sense of her duties as hostess. "Let us put away the dolls and read."

She packed Christabel and her belongings away again, and went to get some books. Annie waited sullenly. Then, as her friend did not come back immediately, she began to fidget.

"Lucy need not have been in such a hurry to whisk her things into the box," she complained. "To look at the red dress won't spoil it, I suppose. I will have another look at it, anyhow!"

She raised the cover of the box and took out

the dainty dress. Still Lucy did not return. A temptation came to Annie. Why not keep the pretty red silk frock? Lucy would not miss it at once; afterward she would think she had mislaid it. She would never suspect the truth. Annie breathed hard. If she had quickly put the showy bit of cloth back into the box and banished the greedy wish, all would have been well; but instead, she stood thinking and turning the little dress over and over in her hands. In the meantime a hospitable thought had occurred to Lucy. She remembered that there was a new supply of apples in the pantry, and she had gone to get one for Annie and one for herself. On her way through the dining room, she happened to look out of the window.

"Goodness gracious!" she exclaimed; for there was Mrs. Conwell coming home!

At Lucy's call of "Annie, here comes your mother!" Annie started, hesitated, glanced at the box, and—alas!—crammed the red silk frock into her pocket. Then she caught up her coat and hood, and rushed down the stairs. Lucy ran to open the yard gate for her and thrust the apple into her hand as she passed.

Flurried and short of breath, she reached home just as Mrs. Conwell opened the front door. She did not hasten as usual to greet her mother; instead, she hurried to her own little room, shut herself in, and sat down on the bed to recover from her confusion.

As her excitement gradually died away, she found that, instead of feeling the satisfaction she expected in having spent the afternoon as she pleased and escaping discovery, she was restless and unhappy. Upon her dresser lay the apple which Lucy had given her. It was ripe and rosy, but she felt that a bite of it would choke her. Above the head of the bed hung a picture of the Madonna with the Divine Child. Obeying a sudden impulse, she jumped up and turned it so that it faced the wall.

Glancing cautiously around, as if the very walls had eyes and could reveal what they saw, she drew from her pocket the red silk frock. She sat and gazed at it as if in a dream. It was as pretty as ever, yet it no longer gave her pleasure. She did not dare to try it on Clementina; she wanted to hide it away in some corner where no one would ever find it. Tiny as it was, she felt that it could never be successfully concealed. Remorse would point it out wherever it was hidden. Annie began to realize what she had done. She had stolen! She, Annie Conwell, had taken what did not belong to her! How her cheeks burned! She wondered if it had been found out yet. What would Lucy say? Would she tell all her friends? Would they avoid her, and whisper together when she was around, saying, "Look out for Annie Conwell! She is not to be trusted."

She covered her face with her hands, and burst into tears. And all the while a low voice kept whispering in her heart with relentless persistency until human respect gave way to higher motives. She glanced up at the picture, turned it around again with a feeling of sorrow, and, humbled and contrite, sank on her knees in a little heap upon the floor.

A few moments afterward her mother's step sounded in the hall. When one finds a little girl's coat flung on a chair and stumbles over a hood on the stairs, it is clear that the owner has come home in a hurry.

Mrs. Conwell had, therefore, discovered Annie's disobedience. She threw open the door, intending to speak to her; but the sight of the child's flushed and tear-stained face checked the words upon her lips.

"What is the matter, Annie?" she asked sternly.

"O Mother, please don't scold me! I'm unhappy enough already," faltered Annie, beginning to cry.

Then, since the burden of her miserable little secret had become unendurable, she told the whole story. Mrs. Conwell looked pained and grave, but her manner was very gentle as she said: "Of course, the first thing for you to do is to return what you have unjustly taken."

Annie gave a little nervous shudder. "What! go and tell Lucy I stole her doll's red silk dress?" she exclaimed. "How could I ever!"

"I do not say it is necessary to do that," answered her mother. "But you are certainly obliged to give it back. I should advise you to take it back without delay, and have the struggle over."

Mrs. Conwell went away, leaving the little girl to reflect upon the matter. But the more Annie debated with herself, the more difficulty she had in coming to a decision. Finally she started up, exclaiming, "The longer I think about it, the harder it seems. I'll just do it right now."

She picked up the dress, darted down the stairs, hurriedly prepared to go out, and in a few moments was hastening down the block to the Caryls'. Lucy saw her coming, and met her at the door.

"Did you get a scolding? Was your mother upset?" she asked; for she saw immediately that Annie had been crying.

"Oh, no!—well, I suppose she was," hesitated Annie. "But she did not say much."

"How did she happen to let you come here again?" continued Lucy, leading the way to the living room.

Annie cast a quick glance at the table. The box which contained Christabel and her wardrobe was no longer there. It was useless, then, to hope for a chance to quietly slip the red dress into it again.

"I'm not going to stay," began Annie. Her cheeks grew red; and Annie, finding herself so uncomfortable, stammered out the truth. "I only came to bring back something. Don't be angry at what I'm going to tell you. I took that red silk dress home with me; but here it is, and I'm sorry, Lucy, indeed I am!"

After the first surprise, Lucy thought that it must have required a good deal of moral courage to openly bring back the little dress. For a few moments there was an awkward silence; then she managed to say, "Oh, that is all right! Of course, I would have been angry if you had not brought it back, because I would have missed it as soon as I opened the box. I was mean about it, anyway. I might have let you take it to try on Clementina. Here, I'll give it to you now, to make up for being stingy."

Annie shook her head, and refused to take the once-coveted gift from her companion's hand.

"Then I'll lend it to you for ever and ever," continued Lucy, impulsively.

"No, I don't want it now," answered Annie.

The sense of having done right made Annie's heart light and happy as she ran home. She was even happier on the next Saturday afternoon as she knelt in church after receiving the Sacrament of Penance. The experience had taught her that one must learn to see many pretty things without wishing to possess them; and also that small acts of disobedience may lead further than one at first intends.

Annie became an obedient daughter and a most self-sacrificing woman; she never forgot "that red silk frock."

—Adapted from a story written in 1893

Lesson 4: Purpose of Amendment

PREPARATION   To prepare for this lesson, please read pages 445–450 in *The Faith Explained.*

"When we say to God, 'I am sorry for having offended you,' it is no mere act of politeness that we are performing. It is not a dutiful bit of courtesy. Our heart must be in our words. Quite simply, we must mean what we say. It does not follow that we must necessarily *feel* our sorrow. Like love, sorrow is an act of the will, not an upsurge of emotion. Just as we may love God quite genuinely without *feeling* our love, so too we may have a very solid sorrow for our sins without having it cause any emotional reaction. If we are quite honestly determined to abstain, with the help of God's grace, from anything that might seriously offend him, then we have sorrow which is interior."

The Faith Explained by Fr. Leo Trese, pg. 446. Reprinted with permission, courtesy of Scepter Publishers, New Rochelle, NY.

THEME   **III** He **made up his mind to go back to his father**. (firm purpose of amendment)

O my God, I am heartily sorry for having offended You. I detest all my sins because of Your just punishments, but most of all because they offend You, my God, Who are all good and deserving of all my love. **I firmly resolve, with the help of Your grace,** to confess my sins, to do penance, and to amend my life. Amen.

 STORY   Read aloud "Suzy's Dragon" on the following pages to illustrate the importance of having a strong purpose of amendment.

EXAMEN   Discuss the different points in the story, particularly how Suzy was discouraged because it seemed that she couldn't beat her "dragon" despite all her efforts. The Sacrament of Penance gives us the needed grace (God's life in us) to be strong and resist temptation. Suzy came to realize that she needed to do her very best in cooperating with God's help to be able to persevere day after day in fighting the temptation to sin.

 PACKET

PAGES 17–20

Direct your child to choose at least three "dragons" to work on, writing them in the spaces provided on the St. Michael Prayer Card. Have him choose the vices he particularly struggles with and the virtues needed to defeat them. Cut out the two sides of the card and glue them back to back to a piece of colored cardstock. Discuss ways to grow in virtue: by praying regularly, asking for the help of Mary and his Guardian Angel, doing good deeds which quickly become good habits (virtue).

Suzy's Dragon

Suzy sat in one of the great windows of the library, writing out her Latin exercises. It was dull work for her, for she yawned and fidgeted and sighed in a very restless manner. Every now and then she would stop in the middle of a line to watch the boys playing marbles on the sidewalk. There was little Kit and Jimmy Grant—what good times they had! Oh, dear! She wished she was playing marbles on the sidewalk, instead of toiling at these tiresome Latin exercises. Nobody had to study as hard as she did, she was sure. There was Tom, now, flying his kite! And there—yes, there was Ellen Hamlin going after trailing arbutus, a type of trailing strawberry plant that has pink and white flowers! This was too great a temptation. Down went the exercises, and up went the window. She called, "Oh, Ellen! Ellen! Are you going after trailing arbutus?"

Yes, Ellen was going after trailing strawberries, and she wished Suzy would come with her. Why couldn't she? Suzy asked herself the same question, and she came to the conclusion that there was really no sufficient reason why she couldn't. "Because I can write the rest of my exercises out tomorrow morning," she thought.

"I'm just going for a walk to the Pinewoods," she said to Aunt Cathy, who had charge of Suzy and her brothers since their mother's death.

Aunt Cathy lifted her kind but penetrating gaze to Suzy's face, and Suzy felt uncomfortable, though all her aunt said in reply was, "Very well, my dear; you know best whether you can spare the time."

This was always Aunt Cathy's way. Suzy was the one who had lessons to learn—and Suzy was old enough to decide when these duties were over, and whether her lessons were learned. And if Suzy wasn't faithful to her duty, she would be the one to suffer.

Suzy always knew when Aunt Cathy thought she had neglected anything, and it always made her feel very uneasy. And now, over this lovely spring afternoon, searching for trailing arbutus with Ellen Hamlin, there was this shadow of uneasiness, of something unfulfilled, which clouded the bright day, and made the pleasure half a pain. But they were very successful in their hunt for flowers. Suzy had never carried home such a big basketful, and dear, kind Aunt Cathy admired them to her heart's content.

"But you look tired, Suzy," she said to her.

"Yes, we went farther than we meant to at the start; we went almost to Long Roads, Aunt Cathy."

"Which is almost three miles. I should think you'd be tired, Suzy. Now I should advise you, my dear, to eat your supper at once and go to bed."

And Suzy was sensible enough to take this advice, for she remembered what she had to do in the morning—and if she should oversleep!

"Will you call me when you get up, Aunt Cathy?" she asked when she went upstairs.

"You want to wake up at five o'clock?" exclaimed Aunt Cathy in astonishment.

"Yes, Aunt Cathy."

"Oh, well, I can do that easily; but it'll not be so easy for you to mind it," Aunt Cathy replied.

It didn't seem more than an hour to Suzy when she heard Aunt Cathy calling at her door, "Come, Suzy, it's five o'clock, and you remember you wanted me to call you."

"Yes, Aunt Cathy, I hear," she answered, "and I'm going to get right up," which she certainly meant to do. But it was so early, so long before seven o'clock, she would lie just a minute more. That was the last she remembered until a great thumping at her door broke into a morning dream.

It was her brother Tom. "Come, Suzy," he shouted, "aren't you ever going to get up? It's breakfast time. Come! Hurry up! I want you to see me fly my new kite. I bought it from Sam Green yesterday; it's the tallest kite you ever saw."

Suzy was horrified. Breakfast time! How could she have slept so long? Only an hour until her exercises must be ready! Was there ever such an unlucky girl? "Do go away, Tom," she said meanly to her brother, as she hurried into the library after a hasty breakfast. "I can't attend to your kite now, I'm in a hurry."

Tom flung out of the room in disgust. "I never saw such a girl in my life as you are, Suzy. You're always in a hurry, and you never get out of it."

She had no time to reply, for Tom had banged the door shut. Then what could she have replied? When the truth is told to us what is there for us to say?

But the fact was at present Suzy didn't think much about the saying; it was the doing that occupied her. Here were two pages yet to translate! She set to work now in good earnest, but of necessity, it had to be very hurried work; and Suzy was never a ready translator. She was always a little uncertain with those perplexing verbs and pronouns. She had no time this morning to go back and correct mistakes, however, for she was only at the foot of the first page when it was time to finish her chores before school.

Poor Suzy! It turned out to be a dreadful day for her. She got a bad mark, for that Latin lesson was an awful boggle, and another for not paying attention during math lesson.

"Dear me!" she sighed, almost in tears. "Everything has gone wrong this week. I suppose it's what Cousin Bella calls Fate."

"What does ail you, Suzy?" asked Aunt Cathy.

Suzy burst into tears. A dim consciousness was stealing over her that the "everything going wrong" wasn't Fate exactly.

Then Suzy told Aunt Cathy her troubles, how it all got worse and worse each day. Aunt Cathy listened gently and patiently, but at the end she did not say much. She felt sure that Suzy was finding out for herself the cause of these troubles, and she thought this would be better for her in the end than to have her fault held up before her by somebody else.

Today, at least, Suzy was on her guard. She took her history lesson into a little back room, where she could neither see the boys playing at marbles, nor Tom flying his kite, nor Ellen Hamlin if she passed. Then she put her mind upon her task, and she was astonished to find that by this steady work, she had finished in an hour what she had many a time spent three hours over.

Suzy went into the parlor and found Aunt Cathy reading aloud to little Kit. It was a pleasant story. After the reading, which both Suzy and Tom had enjoyed as much as little Kit, they all began looking over the pictures in the book. Suzy came across a picture of St. George and the Dragon.

"Who was St. George, Aunt Cathy?" she asked.

"The legend of St. George is that he was a renowned prince, whose greatest achievement was the slaying of an enormous dragon and freeing a princess from bondage. To everyone now it is a symbol of victory of some kind, the victory gained over any weakness or sin, for we all have some weakness or sin, which is a dragon for us to fight."

As Aunt Cathy concluded, Suzy's face grew very grave and earnest; and bending over the picture of St. George, she looked at it a long time in silence; but it was not until she was alone with Aunt Cathy that she spoke what was in her mind.

The boys had both gone to bed, and she still held the picture before her, regarding it with great interest, when she said, "Aunt Cathy, I've found my dragon. It is that long word beginning with 'P,' that little Kit was trying to spell the other day. It means to keep putting everything off until another time that ought to be done right away."

"I know. 'Procrastination'—that is the word, Suzy."

"Yes, that is it; that is my dragon, and it's been the cause of all my troubles, Aunt Cathy. Now I'll tell you what I'm going to do. I'm going to ask Father if he will let me have this picture, and I'll hang it at the foot of my bed, and try to remember when I say my prayers that I've got a battle to fight every day, for I have, Aunt Cathy. Oh, you don't know what hard work it is for me to sit and study. If it isn't one thing, it is another that makes my mind wander. And then, at the end of an hour I don't know a word of my lesson. Somebody will call for me to go somewhere, and I think, 'Oh, well, I can finish the lesson tomorrow.' And then when tomorrow comes, all sorts of things will happen, so there won't be a bit of time. That's the way the dragon has gone on beating me, ever and ever so long and—I don't know, Aunt Cathy, but—but he always will." And here Suzy began to choke a little. The next moment she burst out bravely in a determined voice, "But I shall keep trying very hard to beat him, anyway."

"That's it, Suzy!" Aunt Cathy exclaimed. "Try 'very hard,' and with God's help, I know you will win the battle, my dear."

And Suzy was true to her word. She did try "very hard," and with God's help she at last won the battle.

—Adapted from a story written in 1866

Habits

"How shall I a habit break?"
As you did that habit make.

As you gathered, you must lose;
As you yielded, now refuse.

Thread by thread the strands we twist
Till they bind us neck and wrist;

Thread by thread the patient hand
Must untwine 'ere free we stand.

But remember, as we try,
Lighter every test goes by;

Wading in, the stream grows deep
Toward the current's downward sweep;

Backward turn, each step towards shore
Shallower is than that before.

—John Boyle O'Reilly

Lesson 5: Confession of Sins

PREPARATION

PREPARATION

To prepare for this lesson, please read pages 451–453 in *The Faith Explained*.

"Another noteworthy blessing of confession as a part of the sacrament of Penance is that it provides us with skilled advice in our spiritual problems. Just as we obtain from the physician expert help in the cure and prevention of our physical maladies, so too we find in confession one who is learned in the ills of the soul, one who can prescribe the remedies and safeguards that will contribute to spiritual health and growth in holiness."

The Faith Explained by Fr. Leo Trese, pg. 453. Reprinted with permission, courtesy of Scepter Publishers, New Rochelle, NY.

THEME

IV He **confessed** his sins.
(tell our sins to a priest)

O my God, I am heartily sorry for having offended You. I detest all my sins because of Your just punishments, but most of all because they offend You, my God, Who are all good and deserving of all my love. I firmly resolve, with the help of Your grace, **to confess my sins,** to do penance, and to amend my life. Amen.

 STORY

Read aloud "What a Dollar Bought" on the following pages to reinforce the necessity of confessing our sins to a priest.

EXAMEN

Discuss the different points in the story. Why did Dick give up his first Christmas dollar? Was Dick's sacrifice easy? Could Dick have made this great sacrifice unless he had already been living his life for God? By giving up his dollar, Dick showed that he loved God and the man more than what he could buy with his dollar.

Did God "turn His back" on the old man?

Could Dick's money buy anything more valuable than the forgiveness of a person's sins? Did Dick truly end up "laying out his Christmas dollar in love"?

 PACKET

PAGES 21–22

The Confession Card can serve as a reminder to your child to go to confession on a regular basis, and how to prepare for it. Cut out the two sides of the card and glue them back to back to a piece of colored cardstock. Invite your child to decorate and keep the card in a handy place.

What a Dollar Bought

"Good-bye, my son, and God bless you," said Father John, heartily, as he took his bag from Dick. "And here's a dollar for Christmas." With these words the good priest, who had been making his half-yearly visit to the little mission chapel in the mountains, sprang onto the train and was carried away into the gray, wintry twilight.

For a moment Dick stood staring, fairly struck dumb. A dollar! a whole dollar!—the first that Dick had called his own in all his fourteen years of life. True, he had earned honest wages, but they had come to him only in the shape of food and bed at the Hutchins' farmhouse, coarse homespun clothes, and an occasional pair of shoes.

Dick was an orphan, whom good Mother Hutchins had taken from the orphanage. Just before our story opens, the kind old woman died; a daughter-in-law had come to rule in her stead, and now life was far from pleasant at the farm.

But there was always a roaring fire in the farmhouse kitchen, plenty on the farmhouse dinner table, and outside the wild, sweet freedom of the woods and the hills.

Twice a year Father John came, and Dick, by virtue of the good Sisters' training in the orphanage, became a very important person. It was he who scoured the woods for greens or flowers to deck the little altar, he who lighted the candles, served the Mass, and was sexton, sacristan, and master-of-ceremonies all combined.

"I hope Father John didn't mean this for—for—pay," said Dick, a sudden flush of honest pride coloring his face as he looked at his dollar. "But he didn't—I know he didn't—he said it was for Christmas. But," continued Dick, shaking his head, "Father John shouldn't be throwing money around like this. There was a hole in his cassock and two patches on his boots—and—and—but I can't get it back to him now, so I'm going to do what he says: spend it for Christmas."

Christmas had never before presented any serious problems to Dick, but now matters were different. He stopped at the window of the village store where, amid an array of dolls, drums, and woolly dogs, lay three pairs of skates.

"My, but they are beauties!" murmured Dick.

"Hallo! is that you, Dick?" said a voice at his elbow, and Si Green's freckled face looked out from homemade cap and coat. "Snapping weather, isn't it?"

"Fine," answered Dick, heartily.

"Maybe you think so. You wouldn't if you were I," answered Si, peevishly. "I can't go sledding or skating or anything, on account of this throat of mine."

"What, never again?" exclaimed Dick.

"Not this winter," was the hopeless answer. "Just when I had painted up that double runner of mine, and got her in prime order. I've a mind to sell her."

"What will you take?" asked Dick, his heart giving a sudden leap, for Si Green's double runner was the admiration of every boy on the Ridge.

"One dollar cash and not a cent less. It's worth more, but Jake Bond has an accordion that I'd like to have. It cost five dollars when it was new, but Jake says he will sell it for a dollar."

Dick fairly lost his breath. An accordion! Something to make music had been one of the dreams of his young life. He had sung, whistled, played the mouth-organ, but an accordion had been quite beyond his wildest hopes.

"Si," he faltered, "Si, would you feel very bad if I bought that accordion? I'd lend it to you whenever you wanted it; I'd come up here and play for you until you saw a chance of getting another. I've got a dollar—"

"You have!" said Si. "Where—where—did you get it?"

"It's a Christmas gift from Father John," was the proud reply.

"My! my!" gasped Si. "But I say, Dick, you can get an accordion almost any time. If I were you, I'd rather have Dave Whiting's pup. Prettiest thing you ever saw, real Newfoundland, all covered with soft, black, curly hair, and full of tricks already. Dave said he wouldn't take ten dollars for him, but his folks have sent for him to come to town on New Year's, and he wants cash."

Dick's mind took another turn. A dog! A black, curly, leaping, frisking, four-footed chum that could live in the stable yard and feast on bones! Poor, lonely, orphan Dick's heart gave a jump of delight at the very thought. "Where can I see him?" he asked.

"Down at Cissel's," answered Si. "Dave is staying there, and you'd better strike a bargain, if you can."

Dick started off for the Cissel farm, a Christmas thrill in his breast, as he thought of all the new delights that had suddenly come within his reach.

"Skates, sled, accordion, or pup! I can have any one of them. It's pretty hard to choose. But the pup!" Dick drew a long breath of delight. "A black, curly fellow, licking my hand and jumping at my call and running to my whistle, watching for me and loving me—that's the best of all. I'll just lay out that Christmas dollar in love, if it's only a dog's." Dick quickened his steps and wheeled briskly around the turn of the road that led past the little mission chapel, which was locked and deserted now after its three days of warmth and light.

As he stopped to look at the building, he caught sight of a figure apparently skulking near the arched doorway. "Hello!" he cried quite fiercely. "Come out of there. I am in charge of this church."

The figure came forward. It was an old, gray-haired man, shabby and forlorn.

"You're in charge you say, lad? Then let me in—let me in. It's a sore burden I'm bringing to the foot of God's altar. Let me in to the priest."

"The priest!" echoed Dick. "He isn't here."

"Not here," repeated the old man in a trembling voice. "Sure they told me at the Gap he was holdin' a station here."

"He was," answered Dick. "But he has gone."

"O dear, O dear!" moaned the old stranger; "I've walked twenty miles this day to find him—I that haven't been to confession this forty years—"

"Forty years—whew!" exclaimed Dick. "It's about time you were squaring things up—"

"It is, it is," continued the trembling speaker; "and bitter years they have been. I've come now to make my peace with Heaven. But the just God has turned His back on me—I must die as I've lived. It's too late."

"Oh, look here, none of that," said Dick. "It's never too late, you know. Father John was preaching about that last night. He is going to stop at Flynn's station about fifteen miles from here—until tomorrow morning, and if you get on the next train you can catch him there."

"The next train," repeated the old man. "How can a poor beggar like me get on the train? Didn't I tell you I walked every foot of the way here? There's nothin' for me to do but to go back as I came."

A sudden thought flashed into Dick's mind; for a moment there was a fierce struggle in his breast. Then his hand went down into his pocket and brought out his Christmas Dollar.

"Here, take this," he said. "It will pay your way to Flynn's and back—"

"God bless you—it will, it will," almost sobbed the old man. "It is God's own angel that is opening the way for me."

"Lean on me," said Dick, a little huskily; there was a big lump in his throat, for he knew that skates, sled, accordion, and puppy all were gone. "Lean on me and move lively, and you will catch the 8:30 train. Come on."

Months afterward, Dick, coming home from work one day, saw a familiar figure on the porch.

"Father John!" he exclaimed delightedly.

"Yes," was the cheery answer. "You didn't expect me so soon, but I've come on business—to pay interest on that little investment you made last Christmas."

"Sir?" said Dick, staring into the speaker's face.

"The man you sent to me with your Christmas dollar died last week in God's peace, thanks to your charity, Dick—and he made you his heir. He had only a poor little shanty on a few acres of rock, and at first I thought your property was not worth claiming. But it seems the railroad has been trying to buy it for the last ten years, and the old man refused to sell. Now they offer you two thousand dollars for it. You can go to school now, Dick, and with God's help, you will grow to be a fine young man."

And a fine man indeed Dick became. On Christmas Day his beautiful home is bright with love and cheer. His own merry boys and girls gather around the tree laden with toys and gifts, not only for them but also for every poor little orphan child within his reach. And his thoughts go back tenderly to that far-off past, and he tells another curly-haired little Dick, who nestles at his side, the story of his first Christmas dollar.

—Adapted from a story written in 1800s

Lesson 6: Penance

PREPARATION   Recommended reading: pgs. 463–468 in *The Faith Explained*

"It should be remembered that the penance prescribed for us in confession has a special efficacy in paying our debt of temporal punishment because it is a part of the Sacrament of Penance. We should, of course, perform other penitential works on our own. All our meritorious works can be offered as satisfaction for our sins, and should be so offered. This does not mean only the prayers we say, the Masses we offer, the acts of religion or charity that we perform. It means every single action of our Christ-centered day; that is, every action (barring bad actions, of course) that is done in the state of grace and from a sense of duty to God. These are the actions that gain merit for us in heaven and at the same time can be offered in satisfaction for sin."

The Faith Explained by Fr. Leo Trese, pg. 467. Reprinted with permission, courtesy of Scepter Publishers, New Rochelle, NY.

THEME

V   He was **ready to do anything his father said**.
(do the penance the priest gives us)

O my God, I am heartily sorry for having offended You. I detest all my sins because of Your just punishments, but most of all because they offend You, my God, Who are all good and deserving of all my love. I firmly resolve, with the help of Your grace, to confess my sins, **to do penance, and to amend my life. Amen.**

 STORY

Read aloud "The Broken Flowerpot" beginning on page 27 to encourage making up for our sins.

EXAMEN

Have you ever stood by a clear creek or pool and thrown in a pebble to see the ripples? The ripples grow wider until they are far away from the center where you first threw in the rock. Just so do our sins, however small, affect everyone. Sin harms us most, yes, but it hurts all those around us, too. On the other hand, our good actions also have a ripple effect and help everyone.

Discuss how the boy in the story made up for breaking the flower pot.

"It should perhaps be pointed out that *none* of our penitential works would have any value in the eyes of God if it were not that Jesus Christ already has made atonement for our sins. The atonement made by Jesus on the Cross is infinite—more than enough to pay the entire spiritual debt to mankind. But God by positive design wills that we should share with Christ in his work of satisfying for sin. God makes the application of Christ's merits to our own debt of temporal punishment dependent upon our willingness to do penance ourselves. The real value of our personal penances is insignificant in God's sight; but their value swells to a tremendous worth because of their union with the merits of Jesus."

The Faith Explained by Fr. Leo Trese, pgs. 467–468. Reprinted with permission, courtesy of Scepter Publishers, New Rochelle, NY.

Lesson continued on next page >>

 **PACKET**

PAGES 23–24

When the time for your child's First Confession draws near, keep the focus on sorrow for sin and the great joy of receiving forgiveness and grace, instead of on worrying about what to say. Of all the steps to making a good confession, that of true sorrow for our sins is the most important. A bookmark for use during the child's First Confession, and also during the first few months or year afterward, can help keep his focus on a loving encounter with Jesus in the sacrament. Your child can bring the bookmark to confession as long as he finds it reassuring. Freeing the child from distractions ("Will I remember the Act of Contrition?" "How do I start?") will allow him to pay close attention to Jesus' great act of love in the Sacrament of Reconciliation.

Have your child cut out the two sides of the bookmark and glue them back to back to a piece of colored paper. The back of the bookmark is a basic outline of the procedure for confession. This serves as a reminder for the child who may not be comfortable enough to "do it on his own."

The value of hands-on activities while teaching our Faith is in the many opportunities for discussion they provide. As you help your child make his bookmark, discuss and welcome any questions he may have about going to confession. Contrition for sin does not mean we need to look sad, sound sorrowful, or weep! It does mean we don't like the sin, we realize it was bad, we are going to try our best not to do it again, and we are going to make up for the wrong.

Your child can also use the bookmark while he practices going to confession (see activity below).

ACTIVITY   Practice the procedure of going to confession with your child:

> "In preparing my son for his first confession I thought it would be helpful to act out what takes place in the confessional, but I wasn't sure how to hold his interest. Here is what proved successful: First I let him 'build' the confessional using chairs and whatever else he thought necessary, allowing as much time as he wanted. Then, to start out, I let him be the priest. I 'confessed' first and his younger sisters were eager to be included so they were next, trying to follow my example, while I coached my son on what the priest would say and do. He was then eager to show his sisters how a 'big kid' would confess so he took his turn without reserve. We did this weekly as his first confession approached. It was a great success!" *(from a mom of five in California)*

While practicing the procedure of going to confession (see box above), emphasize two things: 1) The sacrament of God's mercy and healing is a positive—not a negative—action. We meet Jesus, He heals us and draws us closer to Him, and He gives us the strength to say "no" to sin. 2) The essential requirement for confession is sorrow for our sins. We may at times become flustered and forget how to say the Act of Contrition, what to do next, and so on. This is normal. Try to keep the focus on being *sorry for having offended God.*

The Broken Flowerpot

One fine day in summer, my father was seated on the lawn before the house, his straw hat over his eyes, and his book on his lap. Suddenly a beautiful blue and white flowerpot, which had been set on the windowsill of an upper story, fell to the ground with a crash, and the fragments clattered 'round my father's legs.

"Dear, dear!" cried my mother, who was on the porch. "My poor flowerpot that I prized so much! Who could have done this?" I popped my head out of the window that had been the scene of the accident.

"Oh," said my mother, mournfully, "I would rather have lost all the plants in the greenhouse in the great blight last May; I would rather the best tea set were broken! The poor geranium I grew myself, and the dear, dear flowerpot which you bought for me on my last birthday!"

Coming out of the house as bold as brass, I said in a shrill voice, "I did it, Mama; it was I who pushed out the flowerpot."

My father had very deliberately taken off his hat, and was regarding the scene with serious eyes, wide awake. I suddenly felt very uneasy as his face grew sterner.

"Well," said my mother, "I suppose it was an accident: be more careful in the future, my child. You are sorry, I see, to have grieved me. There is a kiss."

"No, Mamma, you must not kiss me; I don't deserve it. I pushed out the flowerpot on purpose."

"And why?" said my father, walking up. By this time I trembled like a leaf. "For fun," said I, hanging my head; "just to see how you'd look, Papa; and that's the truth of it. Now punish me—do punish me!"

My father threw his book down, stooped down, and caught me to his chest. "Son," he said, "you have done wrong; but remember all your life that your father thanked God for giving him a son who spoke truth in spite of his fear!"

Not long after this I received a present of far greater value than are the gifts usually given to children. It was a beautiful, large, ivory domino box. This domino box was my delight. I was never weary of playing dominoes, and I slept with the box under my pillow.

"Ah!" said my father one day, when he found me playing with the ivory pieces. "Ah! you like those better than all your other playthings, eh?"

"Oh, yes, Papa."

"And you would be very sorry if your mother were to throw your box out of the window and break it, for fun?"

I looked at my father, and made no answer.

"But perhaps, you would be very glad," he continued, "if you could change the domino box into a beautiful geranium in a beautiful blue and white flowerpot that you could have the pleasure of putting on your mamma's window sill?"

"Indeed I would," said I, wanting to cry.

"My dear boy, I believe you; but good wishes do not mend bad actions—good actions mend bad actions."

So saying, he shut the door and went away. I can not explain just how puzzled I was as I tried to understand what my father meant. But I know I played no more dominoes that day.

The next morning my father found me seated by myself under a tree in the garden; he paused, and looked at me very steadily with his grave, bright eyes.

"My boy," said he, "I am going to walk to town; will you come? And, by the by, fetch your domino box; I would like to show it to a person there."

I ran in for the box, and proud to be walking with my father, I set out with him.

"Papa," said I on the way, "how can my domino box be changed into a beautiful geranium and a blue and white flowerpot?"

"My dear," said my father, leaning his hand on my shoulder, "everybody who is in earnest to be good carries two gifts about with him—one here," and he touched my forehead; "one here," and he touched my heart.

"I don't understand, Papa," said I thoughtfully.

"I can wait until you do, my boy," said he.

My father stopped at a gardener's, and after looking over the flowers, paused before a large double geranium. "Ah, this is finer than the one your mamma was so fond of. What is the price of this, sir?"

"Only seven shillings and sixpence," said the gardener.

My father buttoned up his pocket. "I cannot afford it today," replied my father gently, and he walked out.

On entering the town, we stopped again at a crockery store. "Have you a flowerpot like the one I bought some months ago? Ah! Here is one marked three shillings and sixpence. Yes, that is the price. Well, when your mamma's birthday comes again, we must buy her another, my boy. We have yet some months to wait. And we can wait. For truth, which blooms all the year round, is better than a poor flower; and a word that is never broken is better than a piece of china."

"I have called to pay your little bill," said my father, entering one of those stores in which are sold all kinds of things.

"And by the way," he added, as the smiling storekeeper looked over his books for the amount, "I think my little boy here can show you a very handsome specimen of French workmanship. Show your domino box, my son."

I showed my treasure, and the storekeeper praised it highly. "It is always well, my boy, to know what a thing is worth in case one wishes to part with it. If my son gets tired of his plaything, what will you give him for it?"

"Why, sir," said the shopman, "I fear we could not afford to give more than eighteen shillings for it, unless the young gentleman should take some of these pretty things in exchange."

"Eighteen shillings!" said my father; "you would give that? Well, my boy, whenever you do grow tired of your box, you have my permission to sell it."

My father paid his bill and went out. I lingered behind a bit and then caught up with him at the end of a street.

"Papa, Papa!" I cried, clapping my hands, "we can buy the geranium—we can buy the flowerpot!" And I pulled out a handful of silver from my pockets.

"Was I not right?" said my father, passing his handkerchief over his eyes. "You have found the two gifts of good thoughts and loving deeds!"

Aided by my father, I made the desired purchase, and, on our return, ran into the house. Oh! how proud, how overjoyed I was when, after placing flowerpot and flower on the windowsill, I gently tugged my mother's dress, and made her follow me to the spot. She was speechless with joy when she had learned all.

"It is his doing and his money!" said my father. "Good actions have mended the bad."

—Adapted from a story written in 1886

Lesson 7: Preparation for First Confession

PREPARATION   Recommended reading: "Actual Sin," pages 65–75 in *The Faith Explained*

In order to prepare for confession, you may want your child to memorize a simplified summary of the Ten Commandments: "Think of God, His Name, and day; parents, too, who care for you. Are you kind in every way? Pure, and truthful, honest, too?" Or use "key words" like the ones below:

<u>Honor God</u>,
<u>Honor His Name</u>,
<u>Keep His Day Holy</u>.

<u>Honor and obey parents</u>,
Be <u>kind</u>, <u>pure</u>, <u>honest</u>, and <u>truthful</u>,
be <u>satisfied</u> with what I have, <u>not jealous</u>.

Remind your child that our love is like the wooden beams of a cross. Our love for God is the vertical beam, and our love for others is the horizontal beam.

The more our love for God increases, the more we will reach out to love and help others. To discover how much we really love God, one very simple examen is to look at the way we treat others. We show our love for God to the extent that we love Him in our family members, friends, and neighbors. When we love God, we are loving others. When we love others, we are loving God.

Lesson continued on next page >>

 PACKET

PAGES 25–26

Have your child complete the "Simplified Ten Commandments" project. The vertical beam of the cross in the center is filled with an image of the Blessed Trinity. Help your child to fill the shaded horizontal beam of the other cross with small photos or drawings of family, friends, or neighbors.

The completed page can be trimmed and folded along the dotted lines to form a triangular prism. Staple or tape the two edges of the paper together so it will stand up. Invite your child to place the project on his nightstand as a gentle reminder to examine his conscience regularly.

 STORY

Read aloud "Did You Say *Mortal* Sin?" beginning below to explain the difference between mortal and venial sin.

 PACKET

PAGE 27

Now that your child has studied and discussed the different sections in the Child's Examen as explained on page 7 of this book, present him with page 27 of the Packet. After he colors the border he can paste it onto colorful cardstock and display it in a prominent place.

Did You Say *Mortal* Sin?

Sunday morning, just before it was time to begin Mass, Ellen came into the sacristy. "Father, could I please go to confession?" she asked. "I want to receive Holy Communion but I committed a mortal sin this morning. I got angry at my brother for spilling milk on my clean dress, and I called him some names." I assured Ellen that I would hear her confession if it really was necessary, but that first I wanted to ask a few questions.

"When you got angry with your brother, Ellen," I inquired, "did you get angry on purpose? Did you realize that you were angry and say to yourself, 'I don't care. I'm going to keep on being angry'? Did you deliberately try to think of words and names that would make your brother deeply unhappy? Are you holding a grudge against your brother now?"

"Oh, no, Father! It wasn't like that at all!" Ellen assured me. "I just blew my top all of a sudden and said the first thing that came into my mind. And it's all over now. My brother and I are friends again."

"Then you didn't commit a mortal sin, Ellen," I explained to her. "In the first place it wasn't a serious enough matter. You didn't destroy your brother's happiness and you are not harboring a grudge against him. In the second place your anger was not fully deliberate. You lost your temper suddenly without really thinking about it. Kneel down in your pew and make an act of contrition and your venial sin will be forgiven."

I think that there are many boys and girls who, like Ellen, think that they have committed mortal sins when in fact they have not. It is good to have a conscience sensitive to sin. It is good to have a horror of sin and a fear of offending God. However, we are belittling God's love and mercy if we think that every misstep of ours is a mortal sin. God will not depart from our soul and take His grace away from us for some small offense. We cannot push God out of our soul so easily.

Moreover, if we exaggerate the seriousness of our sins and think that a venial sin is a mortal sin, we may become easily discouraged. We may develop the idea that we cannot be good, no matter how hard we try. We even may be tempted to give up trying.

Let's remember that for a sin to be mortal, it must be in a grave matter that we disobey God. Perhaps the word GRAVE should be written in capital letters. It may seem to us that *any* disobedience of God is a grave matter, and in a sense that is so. But, for God to "give up" on us and leave our soul, the matter must be very serious. It must be something that means a lot to God. We can see the difference between a lie, such as, "Yes, Mother, I did all my homework," and a lie which seriously harms someone's reputation, such as, "I saw George steal some money from teacher's desk."

Another important element of mortal sin is that the sin must be intentional. The very essence of mortal sin is that we deliberately choose self in preference to God. What-I-Want is more important to me than what-God-wants. I love myself more than I love God. Knowing that an act or omission is gravely offensive to God, I choose it anyway. This choice of myself over God does not require a long time. It takes only a moment for the human will to make a decision. But it does require that I understand quite clearly what I am doing and that I am fully conscious of the fact that I am parting from God for it to be a mortal (deadly) sin.

We can see, then, that it would be impossible to commit a mortal sin through sudden surprise (like Ellen's anger) or through forgetfulness or accident. It would be difficult, too, to commit a mortal sin if our mind is confused; for example, by worry, by fatigue or sleepiness, or by illness. To say, "I committed a mortal sin, but I couldn't help it," is a contradiction. If I really "couldn't help it," my action would be no sin at all.

I hope that nothing of what I said will be interpreted as meaning that it is only mortal sin which matters and that we need not worry about venial sin. Quite the opposite is true. It is by avoiding all deliberate venial sin that we best guard ourselves against the danger of mortal sin. To anyone who genuinely loves God, any sin will be hateful, including venial sin.

The important thing is that we do not magnify venial sin into mortal sin. We must realize that it is not "easy" to fall into mortal sin. It is within the ability of each one of us, with the help which God will give, to live always in the state of sanctifying grace.

—Adapted from a story by Leo J. Trese

Part Two: Holy Mass

Overview of Lessons 8–16

**"We have the proof of God's love—He has sacrificed
His life for us."**

OUTLINE

The Mass Book Project is designed to prepare your child for receiving his First Holy Communion and to teach him how to assist at Holy Mass. Include your child in all aspects of the project. Templates and images for the project can be found in the Packet and used to create a book by gluing the pages back to back on colorful cardstock, which you can then laminate and bind with rings or ribbon. The Mass book can also be made using a small photo album, which can easily be added to as the child's understanding of the Mass deepens.

MATERIALS

Supplies: Page Templates and Images from Packet

You will find more images in the Packet than are needed for the Mass Book Project because it is essential that your child choose those images that best illustrate the action of the Mass for him. (You may also use any holy cards or photos you prefer.) Describe and discuss each image and how it represents a particular part of the Mass. After your child has chosen an image, invite him to describe how it "speaks" to him. The topics for discussion are endless and in this case, the images are the springboard for an effective study of the Holy Mass.

"When preparing my son for his First Holy Communion, I found the CHC handmade Mass book to be a very effective teaching tool. They stress the importance of including the child in every step of making the book and I couldn't agree more fully. There were times when I wanted to even out the rough edges or influence his picture selections so that they seemed more suitable to *me*, but I tried to sit back and follow the suggestion. The project turned out to be his favorite part of First Communion preparation! When the big day was a week away and our formal preparations were complete, I asked what he would like to review. He then praised the Mass book project 'because of the discussions' that it led to. The *process* of creating the book was so valuable in my son's preparation." *(from mom of five in California)*

Excerpts from *The Faith Explained* by Fr. Leo Trese can be found in each section, although we highly recommend that parents read chapters 26, 27, and 28 on the Mass, Eucharist, and Communion before beginning this project. Familiarity with this material will enable you to teach the subject matter naturally, which is especially important since discussion is a key element of this project. Be fully prepared, so that you can enrich your child's understanding, deepen his appreciation, and increase his love for Jesus in the Blessed Sacrament.

"The Church earnestly desires that Christ's faithful should not be there [at Mass] as strangers or silent spectators. On the contrary, through a good understanding of the rites and prayers, they should take part in the sacred action as persons who are conscious of what they are doing, with devotion and full collaboration. They should be instructed by God's word and be nourished at the table of the Lord's body. They should give thanks to God. By offering the Immaculate Victim, not only through the hands of the priest but also with him, they should learn also to offer themselves. Through Christ the Mediator, they should be drawn day by day into ever more perfect union with God and with each other, so that finally God may be all in all." —The Council of Trent

Liturgy of the Word:

We speak to God. God speaks to us.

Liturgy of the Eucharist:

We give to God. God gives to us.

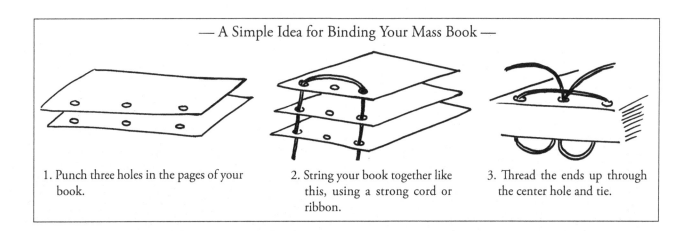

— A Simple Idea for Binding Your Mass Book —

1. Punch three holes in the pages of your book.

2. String your book together like this, using a strong cord or ribbon.

3. Thread the ends up through the center hole and tie.

Mass Book Project Lesson Plan

LESSON 8: FRONT COVER

Parent preparation: "What Makes a Sacrifice?" in *The Faith Explained*, pages 377–382

✂ **Mass Book:** Complete the front cover (page 36 in Book) of the Mass book with your child. Front cover image can be found in Packet on page 29.

✂ **Activity:** Help your child complete the Sacred Vessels Search in Packet (pages 31–34).

LESSON 9: PREPARING FOR HOLY MASS

Parent preparation: "Participating in the Mass" in *The Faith Explained*, pages 406–412

✂ **Mass Book:** Complete pages 2–3 (page 38 in Book) of the Mass book with your child. Page templates and images to choose from can be found in Packet on pages 35–37. Remind your child before Mass what the Mass is and the proper attitude of assisting at Mass.

✂ **Activity:** Complete "Giving My All" Coloring Page in Packet (page 39).

LESSON 10: PENITENTIAL RITE

✂ **Mass Book:** Complete pages 4–5 (page 39 in Book) of the Mass book with your child. Page templates and images to choose from can be found in Packet on pages 41–43.

📕 **Story:** Read aloud "Terrible Farmer Timson" (pages 40–42 in Book).

LESSON 11: LITURGY OF THE WORD

✂ **Mass Book:** Complete pages 6–7 (page 43 in Book) of the Mass book with your child. Page templates and images can be found in Packet on pages 41 and 45. We treasure God's Word and let it come to life in us!

LESSON 12: OFFERTORY

Parent preparation: "Participating in the Mass" in *The Faith Explained*, pages 406–409

✂ **Mass Book:** Complete pages 8–9 (page 44 in Book) of the Mass book with your child. Page templates and images can be found in Packet on pages 47–49.

📕 **Story:** Read aloud "Franz the Server" (pages 45–48 in Book).

Lesson 13: Consecration

Parent preparation: "Bread No Longer" in *The Faith Explained*, pages 358–364

✂ **Mass Book:** Complete pages 10–11 (page 49 in Book) of the Mass book with your child. Page templates and images can be found in Packet on pages 47 and 51. Emphasize that this is the most solemn and sacred part of the Mass.

✂ **Activity:** Read together "My Rocket of Love" and make bookmark (page 53 in Packet).

Lesson 14: Communion

Parent preparation: "So Close to Christ," pages 413–418, and "Practical Pointers for Communicants" on pages 426–431 in *The Faith Explained*

✂ **Mass Book:** Complete pages 12–13 (page 50 in Book) of the Mass book with your child. Page templates and images can be found in Packet on pages 55–57.

Lesson 15: Sending Forth

Parent preparation: Read pages 408–409 in *The Faith Explained*.

✂ **Mass Book:** Complete pages 14–15 (page 51 in Book) of the Mass book with your child. Page templates and images can be found in Packet on pages 55 and 59. We are commissioned to go forth and share Jesus' life!

Lesson 16: Back Cover (Living the Mass)

Parent preparation: "It is for us now to enlarge our understanding of the Mass and to deepen our love for the Mass. It is for us to make more complete the giving of self in union with Christ in the Mass—and to live the Mass by carrying our self-giving into our everyday activities." —*The Faith Explained* by Fr. Leo Trese, pg. 412. Reprinted with permission, courtesy of Scepter Publishers, New Rochelle, NY.

✂ **Mass Book:** Complete the back cover (page 52 in Book) of the Mass book with your child. Page template and images can be found in Packet on pages 61–63. We recommend that you laminate the pages of your child's Mass book for durability.

📕 **Story:** Read aloud "The Parable of Leaven According to Mama" on pages 53–54.

✂ **Project:** If you have time, this would be a good week to invite your child to help you bake a loaf of fresh bread as a wrap-up activity to this section. If possible, make two loaves—one to share with the family and the other with a neighbor or friend who would welcome it.

Lesson 8: Front Cover

PREPARATION   Recommended reading: "What Makes a Sacrifice?" in *The Faith Explained*, pages 377–382

 PACKET

PAGE 29

Mass Book Project: Front Cover   Page 1

Explain the four purposes of the Mass to your child: Adoration, Contrition, Thanksgiving, and Supplication. We offer each Sacrifice of the Mass to adore and praise God, to make up for our sins, to thank Him, and to ask for all the help we need to live as He wants us to live.

The template for the front cover and the cover image of the Mass book can be found on page 29 of the Packet. Point out and discuss elements of the image such as the presence of the Holy Trinity, the adoring angels, and Christ as both Victim and Priest.

"Each individual Mass is not a new sacrifice in which Jesus dies anew. Each Mass is but a continuation, a prolongation through time, of the once-for-all death of Christ upon the cross. To use a modern term we might say that the Mass reactivates for us the sacrifice of Calvary. The Mass makes present and effective for us, right here and now, the Victim on the altar of the cross. The death of Jesus is more than a mere fact of history. It is an *eternal* sacrifice."

The Faith Explained by Fr. Leo Trese, pg. 379. Reprinted with permission, courtesy of Scepter Publishers, New Rochelle, NY.

"The world could exist more easily without the sun than without the Holy Mass."
— St. Padre Pio

PACKET

PAGES 31–34

Help your child complete the Sacred Vessels Search in the Packet. Cut out the images of the vessels and paste them into the boxes next to the appropriate description. See answers below.

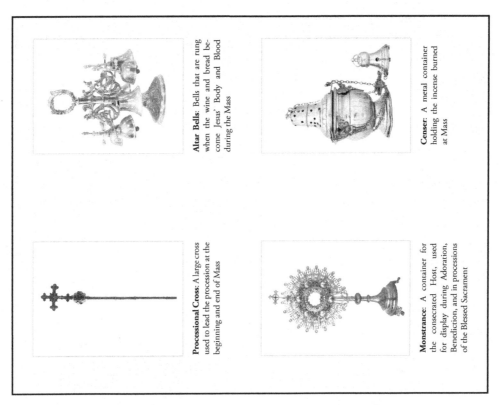

Altar Bells: Bells that are rung when the wine and bread become Jesus' Body and Blood during the Mass

Censer: A metal container holding the incense burned at Mass

Processional Cross: A large cross used to lead the procession at the beginning and end of Mass

Monstrance: A container for the consecrated Host, used for display during Adoration, Benediction, and in processions of the Blessed Sacrament

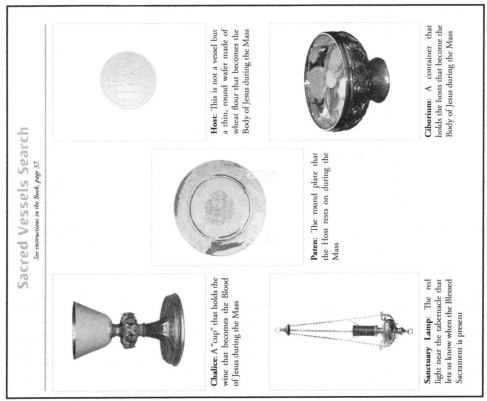

Sacred Vessels Search

See instructions in the Book, page 37.

Host: This is not a vessel but a thin, round wafer made of wheat flour that becomes the Body of Jesus during the Mass

Ciborium: A container that holds the hosts that become the Body of Jesus during the Mass

Paten: The round plate that the Host rests on during the Mass

Chalice: A "cup" that holds the wine that becomes the Blood of Jesus during the Mass

Sanctuary Lamp: The red light near the tabernacle that lets us know when the Blessed Sacrament is present

Lesson 9: Preparing for Holy Mass

PREPARATION   Recommended reading: "Participating in the Mass" in *The Faith Explained*, pages 406–412

 PACKET   **Mass Book Project: Preparing for Holy Mass**   **Pages 2–3**

PAGES 35–37

Complete pages 2–3 of the Mass book with your child. Page templates and images to choose from can be found in the Packet, pages 35–37. Remind your child before Mass what the Mass is and the proper attitude of assisting at Mass.

Page 2, God's gift of love: We recall what the Mass is. The tremendous love outpoured on Calvary is the same love—the same tremendous outpouring—we experience at each Holy Mass.
Image ideas: the Crucifixion

Page 3, My response: Discuss correct behavior during Mass—genuflecting, using holy water, kneeling quietly. Image ideas: a child in prayer

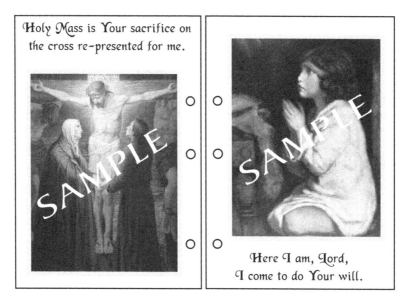

"It is essential for us to remember, however, that participation in the Mass involves much more than mere external conformity to the prayers and the ceremonies of the Mass. Above all else the Mass is an *action* in which we are engaged—with Jesus."

The Faith Explained by Fr. Leo Trese, pg. 407. Reprinted with permission, courtesy of Scepter Publishers, New Rochelle, NY.

 PACKET   Invite your child to color in the "Giving My All" Coloring Page.

PAGE 39

Lesson 10: Penitential Rite

 PACKET   **Mass Book Project: Penitential Rite**   **Pages 4–5**

PAGES 41–43

Complete pages 4–5 of the Mass book with your child. Page templates and images to choose from can be found in the Packet, pages 41–43.

Page 4, God's gift of mercy: Use one of the images for the penitential rite found on page 43 of the Packet.

Page 5, My response: Child may choose an image which reminds him of being sorry for sin. Another idea is a picture of Jesus embracing children—a reminder to go to Jesus for help to be good!

"None of us of course could make adequate satisfaction for sin. But Jesus Christ could, and on the cross he did. Drawing upon that inexhaustible fund of satisfactory merit, Jesus continues to offer it daily to God in the Mass. The infinite value of Christ's satisfaction for sin does not of course excuse us from making reparation ourselves. It is precisely because of the infinite satisfaction for sin made by Jesus on the cross that our own acts of reparation, offered in union with his, have value in the eyes of God. This is the fourth purpose then for which Mass is offered: to make satisfaction to God for the sins of men."

The Faith Explained by Fr. Leo Trese, pg. 382. Reprinted with permission, courtesy of Scepter Publishers, New Rochelle, NY.

 STORY   Read aloud "Terrible Farmer Timson" beginning on the next page.

Terrible Farmer Timson

Jill and Audrey woke up in the farmhouse bedroom on the first morning of the summer holidays. At first they were not awake enough to know just why they felt so happy. Then the sounds and smells of the holidays gathered into the morning: the cock crowing (a scarlet sound like a pennon blown out curling on the wind), the sound of milk cans and hobnailed boots on flagstones, the sound of voices that were slow and burred and spoke words that were brown and velvet like the bees' backs, the smell of grass in the early sun and of clover in the grass.

All day their delight folded and took new shapes: getting the eggs for breakfast and feeling them warm and softly polished in the palm of one's hand, wearing old blue overalls and no shoes or stockings or gloves or hats, picking fruit and eating it out of doors, and at last evening, and night bringing a darkness that was gentle and moved along under the trees in the orchard like deep blue clouds, and stars among the branches like golden fruit.

Jill and Audrey remembered that all the loveliness of the day was God's gift, and then they remembered the promise they had made: that though they were alone, and in the charge of Mrs. Brown, who was not a Catholic, they would ask George Brown to drive them to Mass in the pony cart every Sunday. For tomorrow was Sunday. George, however, shook his head; the pony had gone lame.

Jill said, "It doesn't matter, we could walk."

But Mrs. Brown laughed at the very idea. "It's four miles there and four miles back," she said. "That's eight miles; you couldn't walk eight miles, and what's more, Almighty God wouldn't expect it of you."

Audrey said slowly, "No, perhaps He wouldn't, and anyway it wouldn't be a sin not to go; but really, we *do* walk eight miles in the fields, I'm sure, and if God doesn't expect it, it would make Him all the happier, like giving Him a surprise."

"Course," said George, "if you be that *set* on going,

it is a short cut through Farmer Timson's land, only if he caught you he'd carry on terrible, he don't let no one cross his land; a fair caution he is!"

"Couldn't we ask him?"

"Well, you *could*, but there's no saying what he'd say."

"Well, we'll try," said Audrey, and taking the candle from the kitchen table and holding it above her like a star, she climbed the wooden stairs to the bedroom.

Farmer Timson had had a miserable day. Saturday was always a black day with him. He sat in his little lovely wood and stared through the big leaves, and just because the leaves were all lovely with the light of the evening he was all the more wretched. He picked a wild flower and crushed it between his big finger and thumb; it hurt him to see it looking so frail and lovely when he felt himself to be so rotten. Yes, rotten, that's what he felt! When he was a boy, and even when he was a man, Saturday was Confession day, and he had looked forward to it, yes, looked forward to coming back along the white road into this very wood and feeling that now he was free of all his sins, the flowers and the birds and all the lovely wild things were his friends.

Then the foolish man had quarreled with the priest, a priest who had been dead many years now, and so he had not gone to the church along the road any more. And he had put notices up all around his fences, forbidding people to pass. And everyone had forgotten that old Timson had ever been a Catholic, everyone but himself. He was a fair caution now, as George said, a man with his heart aching for something he couldn't have, just because his own silly self would not let him be humble enough to go and get it. But he was so unhappy that he simply had to pretend to himself that he was very fierce and terrible and didn't mind a bit. When people came to ask him timidly if they might take the short cut through his land, he shouted "No!" so angrily that in the end no one came any more.

On this particular Saturday he was lonelier than ever, so he crushed flowers in his fingers and tried to think of some notice to put up that would be even more alarming than the others. Sitting contentedly in the grass and the white clover, a red cow gazed at him with her quiet eyes. She sat in a field just beyond the wood; so still she was that she might have been one of those cardboard cows that gaze so gently across the manger in the crib at Christmastime.

"Idiot," said Farmer Timson, looking at her. "Idiot!" And when in return for this unprovoked insult she gazed at him all the more softly, lying quite still, he went into the tool shed and prepared a new notice: "Beware of the Mad Bull!"

Audrey and Jill stood a little doubtfully outside Farmer Timson's white gate. It was useless to deny that their Sunday clothes lessened their courage. And when they discovered that they could pass through Farmer Timson's land only at the cost of persecution, their hearts sank. For there in front of them was the notice: "Trespassers will be Persecuted." That is what it seemed to say, but the letters were a little worn with weather and age. Audrey's eyes grew big.

"You've often said," remarked Jill, "that you would like to be persecuted."

"Ye-es," said Audrey doubtfully, "I did use to think perhaps I'd like to be a martyr. I'm sure I would *after* I'd been eaten by the lion, only I've never thought of how it would be *before*."

"Sometimes the lions turn out to be tame, like Daniel's."

"Yes, but not *always*."

"Well, we'd better go on."

They went on to the gate and there in new red paint across the top bars they read, "Beware! Savage Dogs."

"Oh! that's worse than lions!" said Audrey.

"No, it isn't. Dogs don't eat you."

"No, but they bite; and then instead of being a martyr that's forgotten they were ever eaten, you're a bitten person that's not in Heaven."

Jill felt she must stop Audrey talking. "When you aren't worthy to be eaten," she said, "God might be pleased to allow you to be only bitten."

And very firmly she opened the gate. Just then a dog came slowly out of the bushes wagging its tail, a fat, white, smiling dog. "Look," said Jill, "God *is* making the dogs tame. We'd better have more Faith. Come on."

So with the dog trotting beside them, they crossed the first field and came into the small wood. It was very still and filled only with the sound of bird notes and bird wings and the crackling of the twigs where they walked. Their white kid shoes became green with moss and once or twice their dresses were torn on thorns. As to their gloves, they became filthy, but otherwise they went safely, and began to feel quite brave again about martyrdom. But they were unaware that Farmer Timson himself was hidden among the trees at the far edge of the wood.

"You see," said Jill, patting the dog's head, "it's all right after all; there aren't any savage dogs or lions."

"Well, I think," Audrey answered, "that God softened the dog's heart for our sakes, so it may be He'll soften the Farmer's, too."

"Well, George said he is a fair caution."

"Yes, but a fair caution isn't awfuller than a savage dog. Poor old man, I feel sorry for him, being so angry when all the things around him are so gentle."

Farmer Timson, hiding among the trees, scowled. "So I'm being run down behind my back," he thought to himself. But he waited, and suddenly Jill and Audrey stood stock still and gasped.

Audrey spoke first, in a very small voice. "Jill," she said, "do you see? 'Beware of the *Mad Bull*!'"

Jill nodded. Her throat had gone dry. As a matter

of fact, she was a *little* afraid even of cows when George Brown wasn't there. "What shall we do?"

This time Audrey was braver. "Let's pray to God to turn the bull sensible and gentle, and then go on."

"But suppose God doesn't!"

"Then—" said Audrey suddenly, drawing a deep breath and holding it in, "let's go on and offer it up for Farmer Timson to be turned gentle and sensible."

"We-ell," said Jill, doing the same kind of breath, "I suppose we'd better."

Farmer Timson leaned forward among the leaves. Up until now these two children had been just voices to him. Now, very softly, he parted the leaves with his big fingers and peeped at them. What he saw was two small girls who looked smaller still to him because he was a big man.

Jill and Audrey held hands tightly and stepped into the field, just like the martyrs used to step into the Colosseum at Rome. Little girls were an unusual sight in this field and the red cow was an inquisitive old animal. She twitched a fly from her ear, whisked her tail, and prepared to stand up. Audrey and Jill began to run.

Farmer Timson, suddenly overcome with shame at his own mean trick, ran too, out of the green wood, after them. One glance over their shoulder showed a more awful sight than even a standing-up bull. It showed a huge red-faced man, who could be no other than the terrible farmer, in full chase. Jill and Audrey ran the faster. Behind them a voice thundered, "There are *no* savage dogs, there are *no* mad bulls." But "Savage dogs mad bulls" was all that they heard.

They ran on, stumbling on the tufts of grass; their hats blew off and they never thought of picking them up. Farmer Timson yelled again, "There are only kind dogs, gentle cows." But still they ran. Then quite close they heard again, "*Kind* dogs, gentle *cows*," and a huge hand seized each child by the shoulder.

Ten minutes later Audrey and Jill, their hats held very carefully for them by Farmer Timson, were washing their faces under the tap in Farmer Timson's scullery. Then he prepared two mugs

of milk. Certainly God had heard their prayer, for a more gentle and sensible old man they had never met.

"You sit down," he said, "and drink your milk while I get out the pony trap. I'll drive you to Mass and you'll be there in fine time."

"I don't think we're fit to go into church now," said Audrey.

"It's I who am not fit to go," said the Farmer. "Would you believe it, I've let my soul get all muddied up like your dresses and shoes, just because I was too big a coward to say I was sorry to God. But there's time to put that right before Mass, too. So come along."

"You a coward?" said Jill. "I thought you were a caution!"

"Aye, and maybe I was that, too; but when I saw you little scraps going past what you thought was a mad bull because you wanted to help me, I just gave up being a coward and a caution, too. So hurry up now, for the priest is busy on a Sunday and I've got to make my confession before Mass."

—*Adapted from a story by Caryll Houselander*

Lesson 11: Liturgy of the Word

 PACKET   **Mass Book Project: Liturgy of the Word**   **Pages 6–7**
PAGES 41 AND 45

Complete pages 6–7 of the Mass book with your child. Page templates and images can be found in Packet, pages 41 and 45. We treasure God's Word and let it come to life in us!

Page 6, God's Word: Select an image of the Good Shepherd, Jesus preaching, the Sermon on the Mount, or Jesus with children.

Page 7, My response: Child may choose an image of children gathered around and listening to Jesus or one of lambs (which symbolize us) following Jesus.

> "We nourish our souls on the Incarnate Word of God, our Lord Jesus Christ present in the Holy Eucharist. We likewise should nourish our minds and hearts on the word of God as it is presented to us in the words of the patriarchs, prophets, and apostles who penned the words of the Bible. It is the word of God that they present to us."

The Faith Explained by Fr. Leo Trese, pg. 561. Reprinted with permission, courtesy of Scepter Publishers, New Rochelle, NY.

"Speak, Lord for thy servant heareth."
— 1 Kings 3:10

Lesson 12: Offertory

PREPARATION   Recommended reading: "Participating in the Mass" in *The Faith Explained*, pages 406–409

 PACKET   **Mass Book Project: Offertory**   **Pages 8–9**

PAGES 47–49

Complete pages 8–9 of the Mass book with your child. Page templates and images can be found in the Packet, pages 47–49.

Page 8, Jesus' sacrifice: Select a picture of the Last Supper.

Page 9, My response: Like Jesus and Mary, we offer our whole selves to God. Image ideas: Mary offering herself to God, photos of child in prayer, sharing with siblings, helping others.

"What does it mean to be a victim? It means to lay ourselves upon the altar of God's will. It means to say to God, from the heart's deepest abyss, 'Take me, God. I am all yours. Do what you want with me. To live and to labor or to suffer and to die: it is all the same to me, just so your will is done in me."

The Faith Explained by Fr. Leo Trese, pg. 408. Reprinted with permission, courtesy of Scepter Publishers, New Rochelle, NY.

 STORY   Read aloud "Franz the Server" beginning on the next page.

Franz the Server

Tomorrow was the day of the Fair. Tonight Franz stood in the orchard dreaming of the joys of it. All his life, for as long as he could remember, he had longed for the time when he would be old enough to go to the Fair with his brothers, and now the time had come.

Franz pictured it all to himself as Hans and Otto had described it time and again: the noise of it, made up of the band, the hum and jingle of the merry-go-round, the chatter of the people, the students singing. He seemed almost to smell it: the smell of sugared apples, sticks of vanilla, camphor on the seldom-used festival coats, the warm candle grease, the scent on the ladies' gowns, all mingled together with the smell of the clover fields near by, and the clean hot fragrance of the German summer. And then he saw it: the swaying of lights, the great colored bunches of ribbons and balloons, the painted cars and horses of the merry-go-round, the bright stalls, the mountains of gingerbread and sugared cake, the piles of oranges, the flashing of the fairy lanterns, the surging, laughing crowd of merrymakers!

Franz had worked; he had helped Mother to milk the cows, carried in the sheaves for Hans until his arms ached, gathered the fruit in heavy basketfuls for Otto. And now he had his own earned money to spend at the Fair. The joy of it!

Upstairs on the bed his suit was laid out, the red suit with brass buttons that he wore only for Christmas and great days, and new white stockings that Mother had knitted for him last winter. Even now Hans and Otto were grooming the pony and polishing the brass on the trap. They were starting at sunrise, for it was an hour's drive and too much in the heat of the day for the old pony; besides, they must have a long day at the Fair! Franz jingled his money in his pocket. He threw back his head and breathed great waves of the good clean night. He was no baby, he was nine years old and a wage earner, and tomorrow he was going to the Fair.

"Oh, tomorrow, do come!" he cried up to the apple trees. And through the darkness, ringing very clear as sounds do by night, came the clatter of horses' hoofs, over the road, up the drive to the farm house, and stopped at the door. Then came Father's big voice like a trumpet down the orchard: "Franz, come in, the good priest has ridden over to speak with you."

In the farm kitchen Franz saw Father and the priest through the open door. They sat each on

one side of the settle drinking their mugs of beer in the firelight; the dew was all bright on the priest's cloak and his pale face was like brass in the glow of the flames. Franz stood in the open door, his heart beating furiously. He knew what the priest's visit meant.

"Franz," said Father, "you are to ride back with the priest. His regular server has fallen ill and there is no one to serve his Mass tomorrow."

It was not wise to argue with his father, but ... tomorrow! Franz spoke in a very small voice, "I am going to the Fair tomorrow."

"What! After the Father has ridden five miles over the road to take you back! No, no, Franz, you get your cloak and make ready to be off."

Franz looked imploringly at the priest. He was very young; he hardly looked older than Otto, and he smiled at Franz and drew him to his knee. Then he turned to Father. "No, he shall not come," he said. "I will manage without him."

He lifted Franz on his knee, and Franz saw how tired his face was. He thought the priest must have wanted him to come very much, to have ridden so far in the dark when he was so tired.

Franz felt miserable. Somehow a shadow had fallen on the Fair. He never liked serving Mass, and just now he did not like the priest. He made a little movement with his body to show him that he did not like him, and he hoped that Father did not notice it. But the priest did not seem to notice it himself; he only closed his big hand over Franz's little one and smiled at him. Franz wished that Hans or Otto could serve Mass, but he had been taught this year at the same time that the priest had prepared him for his First Communion, and the others had never been taught at all.

Franz remembered, as he sat there trying to fidget in such a way as to show his resentment, that he had once told this priest he would like to be a martyr. Now he felt sure the priest was remembering that, too, and it made him feel more uncomfortable and more miserable than ever. "I can't come," he said, "I just *can't*. I *must* go to the Fair. You don't understand how much I want to go to the Fair!"

The priest answered softly; he really was not at all angry. "Yes, Franz, I do understand. Once I, too, was looking forward to a great Fair. There was going to be every sort of good thing there, and it was going to last for what seemed to me a very long time, all my life."

Franz opened his blue eyes wide. "Forever?"

"No, really for a very short time, just my time on

earth, my one day." He went on answering the questions which Franz had thought but had not asked. "No, I did not go to my Fair. I had another invitation, to go to the great Feast the King had prepared, and I answered that invitation."

Franz knew that the King was Our Lord, and now He was inviting him to come to His Feast. He bit his lips not to cry in front of his father and the priest. He felt very, very unhappy. "It is funny of Our Lord to send His invitations on the days of the Fair," he said huskily.

The priest held his hand more tightly. "It is a very big sign of His love," he said.

"I *can't*," said Franz.

"Very well, He wouldn't want you to come unhappily; neither do I."

When he had finished his mug of beer and pulled his cloak around him, the priest bade them good night and mounted his horse. He had said no more about the server for his Mass, and for a moment Franz felt the weight lifted from his heart. And then, suddenly, he ran down the road and caught up with the horseman. He looked up at him in the darkness. "I want to come," Franz said.

After his long ride through the night air, Franz slept deeply. Just before sunrise the priest lifted him out of bed, still half asleep, and told him to get dressed. He wondered for a moment why he had a dreadful feeling, as if there were a lot of strings tangled around his heart. Then, as he looked out over the fields and saw the little red clouds riding up the sky and the dew golden on the grass, he remembered. Just now Hans and Otto were putting the pony into the trap, or perhaps they had already started.

Heavyhearted, he followed the priest to the sacristy. He lit the candles sadly; how pale and faint their tiny flames looked. Franz thought of the great swinging lamps at the Fair.

They stood at the foot of the altar. "In the name

of the Father and of the Son and of the Holy Ghost," said the priest. "I will go unto the altar of God."

"To God, Who giveth joy to my youth," said Franz miserably.

The priest was saying the *Confiteor*. "They are nearly there," said Franz inside. "Through my most grievous fault," he said with his lips.

How long the Mass took! Why, the priest was still asking forgiveness. What a lot of forgiveness it needed to go up to the altar of God! "I wonder if Hans and Otto are riding the merry-go-round now," said Franz inside.

"The Lord be with you," said the priest. Suddenly Franz hoped the Lord would really be with him, for he was dreadfully afraid a tear was coming out of his eye. "I am not crying," he said inside. "And with thy spirit," said the voice of Franz.

They went up to the altar of God. Franz felt in his pocket for a handkerchief and found none. "Lord have mercy," said the priest. "I never cry," said Franz inside. "Christ have mercy," said a thin little voice, which must have been his.

The Mass went on, and through the server's head the thought of everything at the Fair went on in a woeful procession. He wondered if he would have won a coconut. Would there be donkey rides? He had meant to buy Mother a bunch of ribbons. Perhaps there would be a hundred stalls, and dogs dressed up like brides! The priest had finished the Gospel. "Praise be to thee, O Christ," said Franz, and his voice could hardly be heard at all.

Then Franz shook himself and stared hard at the altar. The priest was lifting the paten with the little host on it. Franz remembered that he should offer himself with the host, and for the first time he understood that he *could* do that.

"I came to Your Feast instead of the Fair," he said to God. "I didn't want to, but I'm glad I did."

He tried to think of a clearer way to say it, but none came. It came into his mind that there was no one hearing the Mass at all. He wondered if everyone was at the Fair. It seemed odd that he, Franz, who longed to be somewhere else, should be the only person at the King's Feast; it would be unkind not to enjoy it. It almost seemed as if it was prepared only for him.

Franz sniffed rather loudly and wished he had a handkerchief; then he squared his shoulders and tried to smile. "I am smiling," he said to God. He was beginning to be really glad he was there; that smile seemed to help. He felt so sorry for the King Who had no one but himself at His Feast; it made him forget to be sorry for himself.

"Poor God," he said foolishly, but very sweetly. "You mustn't think I would rather be at the Fair." He was holding the cruets as he said this to God, and the dreadful tear he had been trying to keep back slipped suddenly down his cheek and fell into the water. The priest seemed not to see it, but Franz saw that tear gleaming and bobbing in the chalice like a diamond in the wine.

As he turned to put the cruets back, he saw something very strange. Just for a moment it seemed as if there was a huge crowd of people in the church, more than he had ever seen. They were all looking at the chalice which the priest was holding up, and every one of them had a tear shining on his cheek. But what was still more odd was that they were not all German people, but people in all sorts of funny clothes, and some of them were dark-skinned and some of them wore clothes like in the olden times, and right in front he felt sure he saw his old grandparents, who had been long dead. There, too, were his own mother and father, and many of his friends, and numberless people unknown to him, rich and poor and young and old; but each and every one of them had a tear on his cheek, and an odd little smile on his mouth.

Franz turned back to the altar. The golden cup, in which he knew his tear still shone like a diamond, was covered now. As he looked at it, he felt as if a flock of birds had broken into song, in his heart, and they seemed to be singing the words that the priest was now saying: "Come, Thou Who makest holy, Almighty and everlasting God, and bless this sacrifice which is prepared for the glory of Thy holy name."

"Come!" echoed the heart of Franz. "Come!" sang the birds in his heart.

He lifted a radiant face, and he knew that a great multitude lifted their hearts with his. For he, Franz the server, lifted not only his soul to God, but also the heart of Christ, the hearts of all the Faithful (for Christ lives in them all). The poor server, who had not wanted to come to the Feast and yet had come, had brought the world with him.

When the priest turned around and said *Orate, fratres,* he spoke in a clear, strong voice for all the world, "May the Lord receive the sacrifice at thy hands." And when the priest lifted the chalice in his hands and whispered the words of consecration, Franz saw the tear, which he knew now to be all the sacrifice and sorrow of all the world, turn red and disappear, and he knew that it was no more a boy's tear spilt into the water, but the Precious Blood of Our Lord.

That day Our Lord gave Franz his second invitation to His Feast. And he received it this time, not with tears, but with joy. So that, though he had many years to wait, he went eagerly when the time came at last, from the Fair of life to the Feast of God. And offering himself to the God Who gave joy to his youth, he offered in his sacrifice, not his one heart alone, but those of all the people who chose to go to the Fair.

—Adapted from a story by Caryll Houselander

Lesson 13: Consecration

PREPARATION Recommended reading: "Bread No Longer" in *The Faith Explained*, pages 358–364

 **PACKET**

PAGES 47 AND 51

Mass Book Project: Consecration   **Pages 10–11**

Complete pages 10–11 of the Mass book with your child. Page templates and images can be found in the Packet, pages 47 and 51. Emphasize that this is the most solemn and sacred part of the Mass.

Page 10, God's gift of love: Use one of the images for the Consecration found on page 51 of the Packet. Another idea is to make a paper host which opens like a door to reveal a small image of Jesus.

Page 11, My response: Choose an image of Mary at the foot of the cross. "Amen" means "so be it," and at the climax of the Mass, our "Amen" is an act of uniting ourselves with Jesus' sacrifice, just as Mary did.

"In the Eucharist the Church is as it were at the foot of the cross with Mary, united with the offering and intercession of Christ." *(CCC #1370)*

"In fact it is a double miracle: there is the miracle of the change itself from bread and wine into Jesus Christ; and the further miracle by which God supports in existence the appearances of the bread and wine, although their underlying substances are gone—like the face of a man remaining in the mirror after the man has walked away."

The Faith Explained by Fr. Leo Trese, pg. 360. Reprinted with permission, courtesy of Scepter Publishers, New Rochelle, NY.

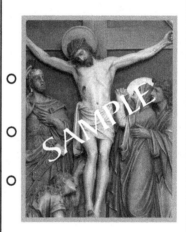

I join my "Amen" with Mary's.

 **PACKET**

PAGE 53

Read together "My Rocket of Love." Show your child how to cut out the images along the dotted lines, glue the two sides together on cardstock and use as a bookmark in his prayerbook.

Lesson 14: Communion

PREPARATION   Recommended reading: "So Close to Christ" on pages 413–418 and "Practical Pointers for Communicants" on pages 426–431 in *The Faith Explained*

 PACKET   **Mass Book Project: Communion**   **Pages 12–13**

PAGES 55–57

Complete pages 12–13 of the Mass book with your child. Page templates and images can be found in the Packet, pages 55–57.

Page 12, God's gift of Himself: Use one of the images for Communion found on page 57 of the Packet.

Page 13, My response: Choose an image showing Jesus coming in Holy Communion. Remember to spend some time in silent prayer with Jesus; adore Him; thank Him; love Him.

"Then there are those precious minutes after Holy Communion, when our Lord Jesus has us, we might say, in His embrace. 'Thanksgiving after Communion' means renewed avowals of love as well as of gratitude. It means a brave asking of the question, 'Lord, what wilt thou have me to do?' and an even braver listening for the answer that will come."

The Faith Explained by Fr. Leo Trese, pg. 430. Reprinted with permission, courtesy of Scepter Publishers, New Rochelle, NY.

"Our Lord does not come down from Heaven every day to lie in a golden ciborium. He comes to find another Heaven which is infinitely dearer to Him—the Heaven of our souls, created in His image, the living temple of the Adorable Trinity."
— St. Therese of the Child Jesus

Lesson 15: Sending Forth

PREPARATION   Recommended reading: pages 408–409 in *The Faith Explained*

 PACKET   **Mass Book Project: Sending Forth**   **Pages 14–15**

PAGES 55 AND 59

Complete pages 14–15 of the Mass book with your child. Page templates and images can be found in the Packet, pages 55 and 59. We are commissioned to go forth and share Jesus' life!

Page 14, God sends us: Select a picture of Jesus carrying His cross, or St. Veronica helping Jesus on the Way of the Cross.

Page 15, My response: Choose an image of children living the Mass (acts of charity and obedience).

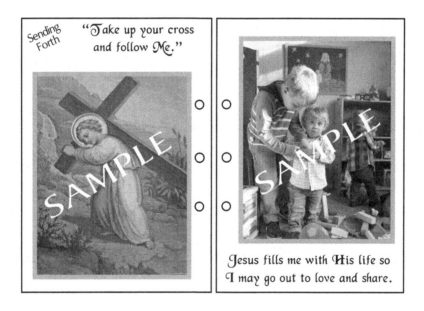

"Besides the wholehearted identification of ourselves with Christ in his role of victim, there is another aspect of our Mass participation which is supremely important. This is the continued in-Mass and after-Mass identification of ourselves with Jesus in the bond of charity. Our affirmation of victimhood would be an empty gesture if we were to negate it by a lack of charity toward any of our fellowmen."

The Faith Explained by Fr. Leo Trese, pgs. 408–409. Reprinted with permission, courtesy of Scepter Publishers, New Rochelle, NY.

"When we leave the holy banquet of Communion, we are as happy as the wise men would have been if they could have carried away the Infant Jesus."
— St. John Vianney

Lesson 16: Living the Mass

PREPARATION

Recommended reading: "It is for us now to enlarge our understanding of the Mass and to deepen our love for the Mass. It is for us to make more complete the giving of self in union with Christ in the Mass—and to live the Mass by carrying our self-giving into our everyday activities." —*The Faith Explained by Fr. Leo Trese, pg. 412. Reprinted with permission, courtesy of Scepter Publishers, New Rochelle, NY.*

✂ PACKET

PAGES 61–63

Mass Book Project: Living the Mass   **Back Cover**

Complete the back cover of the Mass book with your child. Page template and images can be found in the Packet, pages 61–63.

The best gift we can give to Jesus is to do every little thing for love of Him. The back cover is a small reminder to embrace little sacrifices for love of Jesus. Use one of the images for Living the Mass found on page 63 of the Packet, or use another picture which illustrates this idea (holy card of Mary or St. Therese of Lisieux, or picture of child doing a good deed).

We recommend that you laminate the pages of your child's Mass book for durability.

STORY

Read aloud "The Parable of Leaven According to Mama" beginning on the next page.

PROJECT

If you have time, this would be a good week to invite your child to help you bake a loaf of fresh bread as a wrap-up activity to this section. If possible, make two loaves—one to share with the family and the other with a neighbor or friend who would welcome it.

"Today it is your turn and my turn to love one another as Jesus loved us. Do not be afraid to say 'yes' to Jesus."
— *St. Teresa of Calcutta*

The Parable of Leaven According to Mama

Saturday was my favorite of all days because Mama baked bread. In the old days, most every mother baked bread, but no bread could compare with Mama's. Hers was light and crispy, tantalizing to the palate and browned to a golden glow. And the aroma that filled the house made everybody feel happy.

This particular Saturday, I watched her put a tiny cake of yeast into a little sweet water which is always the way she began the dough. "Mama," I asked, "what makes your bread so good?"

She laughed and said, "It's the leaven. Isn't it nice it rhymes with 'heaven'?"

"You bet!" I agreed, "each slice, especially the heel, is like a little bit of heaven ... especially when it's warm and the butter melts down deep." We both laughed a little and then she smiled as if she had a secret. I always loved that smile because I knew she was going to share some of her thoughts

with me. She was good at storytelling. Usually it would be some incident from her own girlhood on the farm or a little tale she remembered from long ago.

I sat back, anticipating some little "parable," as we used to call her tales because there was always a lesson to be learned from them. As I look back now, I realize that Mama had always taught us just as Jesus did long ago, by parables. Usually these anecdotes had to do with the love of Jesus for us.

"See this little cake of yeast?" she began as she stirred the flour into the yeast which had been diluted with water. "It always reminds me of the bountiful love of our dear Lord for each of us. A little is enough to transform all this flat dough into many loaves of bread. Whenever I make bread, I think of the woman in the gospel who hid the leaven in three measures of flour until it raised up and made many loaves."

"Why did she hide it, Mama?" I asked.

"Well, it's like Our Lord's love for us which is often hidden. And, like the leaven, it is a secret force which expands and grows when mixed with the right ingredients. It's often hidden from the mighty and the learned and only revealed to the little ones like you and me, here in this kitchen," she answered.

"Well, how does it work, Mama, to make things bigger?" I asked again.

"It's a chemical reaction called fermentation and when it's mixed with something sweet and something moist like this potato water it rises and expands. If I had no yeast for this dough, the bread would be flat, hard, and have no flavor. It wouldn't rise. None of you children would like it. It would be just like our hearts without the love of Jesus within. We'd become cold and hard and have no flavor for those around us. So, too, when yeast is cold, it won't work. Its action stops. We must never let our hearts become cold to Jesus' love. When we say a little prayer to Him, like 'Jesus, I love you', it works as the leaven and begins to increase and expand in our souls. That is the divine leaven which transforms us into new persons."

We were both quiet a moment. Then hoping she would go on with her parable, and not wanting this delicious moment to end, I asked, "What happens to a person who has no leaven?"

"A person who has no leaven is like a house with nobody living in it," she continued. It has no love, no life, no sounds of children laughing, parents praying, or good smells of baking bread. It is cold and sterile: no activity and no growth. Soon the house begins to deteriorate. The gate becomes rusty, the yard overgrown, the walls begin to get little cracks. Finally it ends in decay. The same with us when our hearts have no love for God.

"Let's take the same house and a young married couple moves into it, bringing the leaven of Jesus' love with them," she continued. "That leaven, now hidden from the world, gradually expands, grows and ferments within the souls of the family that now occupy it. Each new baby adds love and activity. Before long, the house is alive with family sounds; children getting ready for school, doing their chores, parents working together, the family praying together... " Then she laughed and said, "and sounds of broken glass or children squabbling... "

Mama continued her parable. "The leaven spreads throughout the house, increasing and multiplying the love of Jesus. It spreads beyond the house and overflows into the neighborhood and then to the rest of the community. Pretty soon the community is a happier place to live because Jesus is there."

A few hours later, six beautiful loaves of warm bread were turned upside down on the counter. Mama cut me a thick slice of heel and spread butter over it. While I was eating and saying, "Yummm," she finished her parable.

"Remember, Honey, that Jesus has given us Bread of another kind. It has a Divine leaven, one that sanctifies and produces a transformation. Jesus transforms you into Himself through Holy Communion. It is the greatest gift He could give you."

"But, Mama, the holy Host has no leavening. What about that?" I countered.

"Because, my dear, the leaven is within you. I told you that leaven needs sweetening and moistening to make it work. Therefore it is up to you to mix it with the warmth and sweetness of your little heart and moisten it with a few sweet tears of love... then the leaven will start to ferment and act in you until you become more like Him."

"Mama, is there a book about such things?" I loved reading but I never could find a book that could equal Mama for interesting things.

"There's the best book." She pointed to the crucifix on the wall. "It's a book that never stops telling us about the love of Jesus for each of us. It's more eloquent than all the books in the world."

—Adapted from a story by Frances Bodeen

"Every believer, in this, our world, must be a spark of light, a center of love, a vivifying ferment in the dough: He will be so to the degree that, in his innermost being, he lives in communion with God."
— Pope St. John XXIII

Part Three: Preparing Our Hearts to Receive Jesus

Overview of Lessons 17–21

Jesus, come rest within my heart.

INTRODUCTION

This section will help your child to prepare his heart to welcome Jesus. Continue showing your child what a unique treasure the Holy Eucharist is through your words and actions. Your tone of voice and your own reverence and love for God are the best ways to show your child just how awesome and intimate a gift it is to receive Our Lord in Holy Communion!

This season of preparation is important because it gives your child time to develop virtue. A virtue is a good habit. Good habits are formed by repeated good actions. Each act of obedience, charity, or honesty helps your child to form a good habit and grow in virtue. These habitually good acts are done for love of God. Preparing our gifts of love for Jesus can be compared to planting a beautiful garden in our souls—a lovely garden to welcome Jesus.

To introduce each virtue to be practiced, read aloud the story provided in each lesson. After the story is read, discuss practical ways that your child can live the virtue. Use this special one-on-one time to review any questions your child may have about receiving Jesus in Holy Communion.

 PACKET

PAGE 65

During this time of preparing his heart to receive Jesus, your child may color in a heart on the "Gifts of Love" card found in the Packet on page 65 each time he practices one of the virtues listed.

At the end of this time of preparation, let your child wrap his "Gifts of Love" card with beautiful wrapping paper and ribbon. This precious gift may be brought to Jesus during Adoration (Lesson 21) or set on your home altar.

 STORY

To introduce your child to the idea of making gifts of love to Jesus, read aloud the story about St. Therese's "little way" on the next page.

A Story of Saint Therese of the Child Jesus

Adapted from a story by Pere J. Carbonel, S.J.

One time Therese and her sister Celine were sitting together in the garden having an animated conversation in which the word "acts" constantly recurred. This word puzzled a lady who lived next door, and who happened to be sitting at her window.

"Acts, acts!" she repeated. "What do they mean?"

Tired at last of listening, she hurried downstairs to ask Louise, the girls' nurse, what they meant by "acts."

I do not know what Louise told her, or if Louise knew any more about the matter than Madame Battoir herself.

But you, children, shall hear the meaning of this mysterious word "acts."

We can make little sacrifices every day to strengthen us to do God's will. This is called making *acts* of virtue. For example, if a boy does not answer back when he is corrected; if he obeys promptly when he has been told to do something; if he shares with his friends any little treats he has been given; if he speaks kindly to his brothers and sisters; if he tries not to look about in church; if he gives in to brothers, sisters, and friends, instead of always wanting to be first, that boy is making "acts" of virtue.

This is what Celine and Therese were discussing so earnestly. They wanted to make many "acts," and offer them to Jesus. To increase the number and to be able to keep count, they had a special rosary with beads which could be moved up and down. Each little sacrifice was marked by pulling a bead along the string. Therese delighted in this, and was continually to be seen putting her hand in her pocket to count a fresh "act."

Make your own Sacrifice Beads at *http://thelittleways.com/*.

Gifts of Love Project Lesson Plan

✂ PACKET _____

PAGES 67–72 While your child is learning to cultivate specific virtues, begin working on Hand-Made Invitations he can mail or give to friends and family inviting them to come to his First Holy Communion. A number of Eucharistic-themed "cards" can be found on pages 67–72 in the Packet. Or he may use the unused images left from the Holy Mass Project to decorate his cards.

OUTLINE _____

LESSON 17: GIFTS OF LOVE—RIGHT-AWAY OBEDIENCE

📖 Story: Read aloud "No!," pages 58–59 in the Book.

✂ Invite your child to begin using his "Gifts of Love" card (page 65 in Packet), paying special attention to practicing right-away obedience.

LESSON 18: GIFTS OF LOVE—HONESTY

📖 Story: Read aloud "Honesty Rewarded," pages 60–61 in the Book.

✂ Continue with the "Gifts of Love" card by working on the virtue of honesty (acting responsibly in chores and study; truthfulness; good use of time; no tattling).

LESSON 19: GIFTS OF LOVE—SHARING

📖 Story: Read aloud "George White's Ten Dollars," pages 62–63 in the Book.

✂ Continue with the "Gifts of Love" card, working on developing a generous heart by sharing time, talents, and possessions; including others in play; not interrupting; not bickering.

LESSON 20: GIFTS OF LOVE—CHARITY

📖 Story: Read aloud "Jack's Wood Pile," pages 64–65 in the Book.

✂ Continue with the "Gifts of Love" card by working on the virtue of charity (good deeds; thinking of others; being helpful; sacrificial love).

LESSON 21: ADORATION

📖 Story: Read aloud "The Anchoress," pages 67–70 in the Book.

✂ Compile an Adoration Booklet for bringing to Adoration, pages 73–82 in the Packet.

Adoration: Make a short visit to the Blessed Sacrament with your child.

✂ Help your child make a spiritual bouquet as a gift for someone in need.

Lesson 17: Gifts of Love—Right-Away Obedience

Invite your child to begin using his "Gifts of Love" card (page 65 in Packet), paying special attention to practicing right-away obedience.

No!

"A, c-o-n con, Acon, c-a ca, Aconca—Oh, dear, what a hard word! Let me see—A-con-ca-gua. I never can pronounce it, I am sure. I wish they would not have such hard names in geography," said George Gould, quite out of patience. "Will you please tell me how to pronounce the name of this mountain, Father?"

"Why do you call that a hard word, George? I know much harder ones than that."

"Well, Father, this is the hardest word I ever saw," replied George. "I wish they had put the name into the volcano, and burnt it up."

"I know how to pronounce it," said Jane. "It is A-conca—gua!"

"A-con-ca—gua," said George, stopping at each syllable. "Well, it is not so very hard after all; but I wish they would not have any long words, and then I could pronounce them easily enough."

"I do not think so," said his father. "Some of the hardest words I have ever seen are the shortest. I know one little word, with only two letters in it, that very few children, or men either, can always speak."

"Oh, I suppose it is some French or German word; isn't it, Father?"

"No, it is English; and you may think it strange, but it is just as hard to pronounce in one language as another."

"Only two letters! What can it be?" cried both the children.

"The hardest word," continued Father, "I have ever met with in any language—and I have learned several—is the little word of two letters—N-o, No."

"Now you are making fun of us!" cried the children; "that is one of the easiest words in the world." And to prove that their father was mistaken, they both repeated, "No, no, no," a great many times.

"I am not joking in the least," said their father. "I really think it is the hardest of all words. It may seem easy enough to you tonight, but perhaps you can not pronounce it tomorrow."

"I can always say it; I know I can," said George, with much confidence. "No! Why, it is as easy to say it as to breathe."

"Well, George, I hope you will always find it as easy to pronounce as you think it is now, and be able to speak it when you ought to."

In the morning, George went bravely to school, a little proud that he could pronounce so hard a word as "Aconcagua." Not far from the schoolhouse was a large pond of very deep water, where the boys used to skate and slide when it was frozen over.

Now, the night before, Jack Frost had been busy changing the surface of the pond into hard, clear ice, which the boys in the morning found as smooth as glass. The day was cold, and they thought that by noon the ice would be strong enough to bear their weight.

As soon as the school was out, the boys all ran to the pond, some to try the ice, and others merely to see it.

"Come, George," said William Green, "now we will have a glorious time sliding." George

hesitated, and said he did not believe it was strong enough, for it had been frozen over only one night.

"Oh, come on!" said another boy; "I know it is strong enough. I have known it to freeze over in one night, many a time, so it would bear my weight. Haven't you, John?"

"Yes," answered John Brown, "it did one night last winter, and it wasn't so cold as it was last night, either."

But George still hesitated, for his father had forbidden him to go on the ice without special permission.

"I know why George won't go," said John; "he's afraid he might fall and hurt himself."

"Or the ice might crack," said another. "Perhaps his mother might not like it."

"He's a coward; that's the reason he won't come."

George could stand this no longer, for he was rather proud of his courage. "I am not afraid," said he; and he ran to the pond and was the first one on the ice. The boys enjoyed the sport very much, running and sliding, and trying to catch one another.

More boys kept coming on as they saw the sport, and all began to think there was no danger, when suddenly there was a loud cry, "The ice has broken! the ice has broken!" And sure enough, three of the boys had broken through and were struggling in the water. One of them was George.

The teacher had been attracted by the noise, and was coming to call the boys from the ice just as they broke through. He tore off some boards from a fence close by, and shoved them out on the ice until they came within reach of the boys in the water. After a while he succeeded in getting them out, but not until they were nearly frozen.

George's father and mother were very much frightened when he was brought home, and they learned how narrowly he had escaped drowning. But they were so rejoiced to find that he was safe, that they did not ask him how he came to go on the ice, until after tea. When they were all gathered together about the cheerful fire, his father asked him how he came to disobey his positive command. George said that he did not want to go, but the boys made him.

"How did they make you? Did they take hold of you and drag you on?" asked his father.

"No," said George; "but they all wanted me to go."

"When they asked you, why didn't you say 'No'?"

"I was going to; but they called me a coward, and said I was afraid to go, and I couldn't stand that."

"And so," said his father, "you found it easier to disobey me, and run the risk of losing your life, than to say that little word you thought so easy last night. You could not say 'No'!"

George now began to see why this little word "No" was so hard to pronounce. It was not because it was so long, or composed of such difficult sounds; but because it often requires so much real courage to say it—to say "No" when one is tempted to do wrong.

Whenever, in after-life, George was tempted to do wrong, he remembered his narrow escape, and the importance of the little word "No." The more often he said it, the easier it became; and in time he could say it, when needed, without much effort.

—Adapted from a story written in 1886

Lesson 18: Gifts of Love—Honesty

Continue with the "Gifts of Love" card by working on the virtue of honesty (acting responsibly in chores and study; truthfulness; good use of time; no tattling).

Honesty Rewarded

Jean Baptiste Colbert, a boy of fifteen, was busy arranging the rolls of cloth in the shop, when Mr. Certain, who was both his employer and godfather, called him, and said: "I want you to take these pieces of cloth to the hotel to Mr. Cenani, the banker from Paris, who is staying there. The prices, with samples attached, are on these tickets, and you must be careful not to make a mistake."

"Am I to take any less than the prices marked?" asked Jean.

"Not a sou," answered the man. "You are to get the full price, and be sure to bring back the money with you."

Accompanied by a porter, who carried the cloth, Jean went to the hotel, and was shown to Mr. Cenani's room. The banker carefully examined the several pieces of cloth, and putting one aside, said, "I like this best. How much is it?"

"Fifteen crowns a yard," answered Jean. The porter smiled at this, but neither Jean nor the banker noticed him.

"This will do," said Mr. Cenani. "Give me thirty yards of it. I want it for hangings for my library."

While Jean and the porter measured the cloth, the banker walked carelessly to his desk, and taking from it a roll of gold, counted out four hundred and fifty crowns, which he handed to Jean. The lad then wrote a receipt for the money. This done, he and the porter departed.

"Well," said Mr. Certain, as the two entered the shop, "did you make a sale? How did you succeed?

You've made no mistake, I hope?"

"I don't think I have, sir," answered Jean quietly.

"But I do," said the porter, laughing.

"Ah! I might have expected it," cried the merchant, as he hurried to examine the cloth. "But I give you fair notice, you shall pay for your blunder."

"Don't be uneasy," said the porter. "The mistake is in your favor. He sold for fifteen crowns a yard a cloth marked only six."

The merchant's manner changed at once. "Ah! good boy," he said. "That's the way to make mistakes. Fifteen crowns for a six-crown cloth! What a splendid profit! Jean, my dear boy, I am proud of you. You will be a great man."

For a moment Jean could not speak, so astonished was he. But when he recovered from his surprise, "Godfather," cried he, "you surely would not take advantage of this mistake? It is not honest and I, at least, shall take no part in it. I shall go at once to Mr. Cenani, and return the money he has overpaid." And before the merchant was fairly aware of it, the lad was out of the store, and on his way to the banker.

When Jean reached the hotel, he went at once, without being announced, to Mr. Cenani's room, and in answer to the call "Come in," entered. The banker looked surprised and displeased. "What do you want?" he asked. "I cannot be disturbed now, I am engaged. Come some other time."

"Ah, sir!" said the boy, "pardon me, but I must speak to you. By mistake I overcharged you on the cloth you bought, and I come to return you your money," and he laid the gold pieces on the table.

"But you might have kept the money for yourself," said Mr. Cenani, who seemed to forget his hurry, and was now quite interested.

"I never thought of that," answered Jean.

"But if you had thought of it?"

"I could not think of such a thing. It would not be honest," answered the smiling boy.

"You are a fine fellow," said Mr. Cenani, and then asking the boy's name, and inquiring about his family, he dismissed him with the remark, "We shall meet again, Jean, we shall meet again."

On his return to the shop, Jean was met by his godfather, who was in a towering passion. "So this is your gratitude," he cried, as the boy entered, "for all that I have done for you! Leave my sight, and never let me lay eyes on you again." Jean made no answer, but sorrowfully turned his steps homeward. His parents were poor, and, small as his wages were, they would miss the sum, so it was with a heavy heart that he entered the house.

His parents were astonished to see him at that unusual hour. He told, as simply as possible, what had happened, and when he had done, added, "I know not what to do, but I must not remain here idle, a burden on you."

For answer, his mother embraced him warmly, while his father, grasping his hand, said, "Tomorrow we can think of that; today we must think only how we can entertain the noble guest whom Heaven has sent us. For you have acted nobly, my son, and I am, indeed, proud of you."

In the midst of this touching family scene, Mr. Cenani was shown into the room. "I must apologize for this intrusion," he said, "but I leave for Paris early in the morning, and felt that I must see you before going. I have been witness to your son's honesty, and have since learned that by it he lost his situation. I have come, therefore, to offer him a position in our banking-house where we need just such lads as he."

Jean, who had listened in silence to so much praise, his face covered with blushes, now stepped forward. "I am deeply obliged to you, sir," he said, "but my father and mother need me, and as I cannot leave them, I must decline your generous offer."

"But I do not decline it," said his father, tenderly but seriously. "We are very poor, my son. Go, Jean, with this gentleman; in all that concerns the business of your calling, listen to his advice, and follow it; when the principles of integrity and of honor are involved, add to his counsels those of your own heart."

—Adapted from a story written in 1876

Lesson 19: Gifts of Love—Sharing

Continue with the "Gifts of Love" card, working on developing a generous heart by sharing time, talents, and possessions; including others in play; not interrupting; not bickering.

George White's Ten Dollars

George White had been saving his spending money for a long time; in fact, ever since his uncle had given him a beautiful little iron safe, made just like those in his father's office.

One morning he opened his treasure, and on counting it over, he found he had the large sum of ten dollars. "Now," he said, "I can buy anything I want! I must speak to Papa about it."

It was winter, and the ground was covered with ice and snow, so that whenever George went out of doors his mother was careful to see him well wrapped up. He loved to stay out in the open air rather than in the warm house, as his rosy cheeks and bright eyes plainly showed.

He was very fond of skating and coasting, but he had lost one of his skates and his sled was broken. So that evening, as they sat around the tea-table, he said: "Papa, may I spend my ten dollars for a new sled and a pair of skates?"

His father replied, "The money is yours, my son; you may spend it as you please; but tomorrow morning I am going some distance in the city, and intended taking you."

"O Papa, I should like that!"

"Then you must not buy your sled and skates until our return."

George willingly consented; but he could not understand why his father should wish him to wait until they returned, when he could so easily make his purchases on the way.

The next day George prepared to accompany his father; and while his mother handed him his overcoat and fur cap, and wrapped a warm comforter around his neck, he was thinking of the fun he would have with his new sled.

"When I am coasting," he said to himself, "I will lend my skates to Andrew O'Connor, and when I am skating, I will lend him my sled." Now Andrew O'Connor was much poorer than George White, and his widowed mother could hardly afford to buy him toys so expensive. George's resolution, therefore, proved he had a kind heart.

By this time his father was ready for the walk, and taking George's hand, they waved a smiling good-bye. George and his father walked on, passing the splendid houses of the rich, and the large stores wherein are to be found all things rare and costly for those who have money to buy them. Presently they reached a large toy store, where, suspended in the window, was a handsome sled.

Snow-bird, the name of the sled, was on the seat, and the sled itself was painted red and white. "O Papa!" said George, "here is just what I want. Let us go in and get it."

"Wait, my son," said Mr. White, "until we come back."

They walked a little further, and then leaving the bright, gay avenue, turned into a narrow, crooked street, on either side of which were small, dirty, and miserable dwellings, with here and there a tall tenement. Before one of the small houses, Mr. White paused, made a few inquiries, and entered.

George, still holding his father's hand, went slowly up the broken staircase. On the upper floor, they turned, and knocked at a door near the end of the hall. A faint voice from within said, "Come in," and they stepped into the room. The sight that met their gaze would have moved a harder heart than Little George's.

In one corner, on a bed of straw, lay a man feeble and wasted with sickness. Four little half-clothed children, with wan, sickly faces, were trying to play in another corner of the room, and weeping by the sick man's bed sat a pale and slender woman.

George's father spoke to her, and from her lips heard a sad tale of poverty and distress. A friend of his, belonging to the worthy "Conference of St. Vincent de Paul," whose object is to visit the sick in their homes, had already told Mr. White of this suffering family, and he had come to relieve their misery and to see for himself what were their most urgent needs.

He determined to send a doctor at once. George stole up to his father's side and whispered, "O Papa! give them my ten dollars!" When they left the house, Mr. White said, "Are you willing to give up your sled and skates for the whole winter, and spend the money for this poor family?"

"Yes," said George, "I am not only willing, but I want to do it with all my heart."

"Very well, then, my son, you shall buy meat, and bread, and milk, and clothing for the children, and I will take care of their parents."

In the poor room that night were light, and fire, and food, and on the pale mother's face, a happy smile. And George was happier after having done this good deed than if he had bought the handsomest sled and skates in the world.

—*Adapted from a story written in 1876*

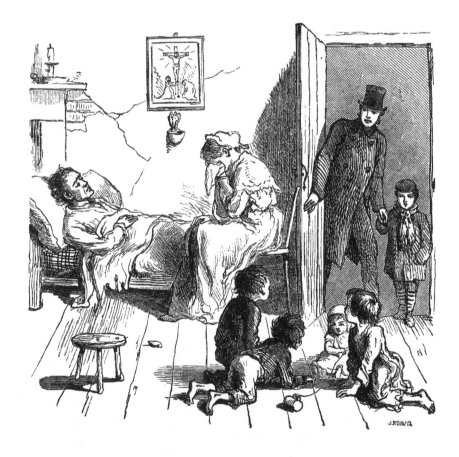

Lesson 20: Gifts of Love—Charity

Continue with the "Gifts of Love" card by working on the virtue of charity (good deeds; thinking of others; being helpful; sacrificial love).

Jack's Wood Pile

"Mother, I think I shall haul the wood down to the village tomorrow."

"Very well, my dear," answered his mother. "I shall have some chickens ready for you to take along."

Since the death of his father, Jack had been the chief support of his mother and his two little brothers. They lived at least four miles from the village, and not a neighbor was within a mile of them, and were it not for the whistle of the locomotive, as the trains passed through the cut below their house, the place would have been lonesome indeed.

Jack was very proud of his wood pile. It had cost him many weeks of hard work, for he had cut and sawed every stick of it himself, and upon it depended the winter's supply of food and clothing for the little family. "I have a cord more than Mother thinks there is," he whispered to his brothers "and with the money I get for that I mean to buy all sorts of nice things—apples and raisins—and maybe Mother will make us some mince-pies for Christmas."

The next day, Jack started with the first load of wood, his head full of plans for extra comforts for his mother and brothers. When he drew up in front of the little store in which the country folks traded their corn, wheat, and other produce for groceries and dry-goods, the owner was standing at the door.

"No, I do not want any wood," he said in answer to Jack's question. "I bought a piece of woodland last summer, and I have cut my own wood this year, and supplied everyone around here.—No, I do not want any chickens, either; but if you are very anxious to trade, I will take what you have

at three cents a pound."

No wood wanted! Poor Jack could hardly keep back the tears; the scarf for his mother, the mittens for the boys, flannels, and other necessities were all gone in a minute. Three cents a pound for chickens! It would pay better to eat them than to sell them at that price. However, he parted with a few to get some things his mother could not well do without, and then turned his mules homeward.

Jack did not unload the wood when he reached home, but left it standing. Snow had been falling for some time, and as the boy walked toward the house, after putting his mules in the stable, the ground was quite white. In a few words, Jack told his mother of his failure to sell the wood, and then seated himself by the fire, resting his head on his hands.

"I do not know what we are going to do," he said after a while, in a tone that spoke more than his words.

"Nor I, Jack," said his mother, putting her arm tenderly round him; "but, my dear, we are not expected to know. It is only Our Lord who knows. We must wait and trust."

"I wonder how things would go on if we would just sit down and trust."

"But we do not sit down and trust. We do our best, and when we have done that, all we can do is to trust. Those were almost the last words your dear father said to me. He saw what was coming, but he felt that God, who feeds the young ravens, would not forget us. Have faith and hope, Jack, my boy, have faith and hope."

The snow fell thick and fast through the night, and the following morning Jack could hardly make his way to the stable to feed the cow and the mules. When he did succeed in getting there, he met a sight that surprised him. In the railroad cut stood a long train of cars half-buried in the snow. A number of men were trying to clear a path before the engine, while, others were passing Jack's load of wood into the cars.

"Halloo!" cried a man who was directing the workmen, "do you know whose wood this is?"

"It is mine," replied Jack.

"Well, if you have any more, I want it,—all you have. Can you bring it here?"

"As soon as I can dig it out of the snow."

"My brakemen will help you," said the man, who was the conductor of the train. "We are in a bad fix. We have been here all night, and are likely to be here all day. My passengers must not freeze. Bring all the wood you can."

Jack hurried to give his mules their breakfast, and while they were eating, he ran to tell his mother the good news.

"Did I not tell you to have faith and hope?" said his mother. "Our dear Lord never forgets those who trust in Him."

Jack worked like a hero that morning, and when he carried the first armful of wood into a car, what a shout of welcome he received from the half-frozen passengers!

"See here," said the conductor, when the fires were well started, "do you know where we can get something to eat?"

"We have plenty of chickens and potatoes and cornmeal, and my mother can cook them," answered Jack.

"And we will help, if she will let us," said three ladies.

Jack's mother and the lady passengers were soon at work, and before long steaming, mealy potatoes, hot cornbread, and delicious fried chickens were served to the grateful passengers.

About noon, the conductor bustled into the

house. "We are off soon," he said, "and I want to square accounts with you. We pay three dollars and a half a cord for wood. Just see what that amounts to. Then there are three or four dozen chickens, bushels of potatoes, and the best cornbread I ever tasted. I am in too great a hurry to figure it all out, but I guess this will pay for it," laying some bank-notes on the table. "If that is not right, just send to the address on this card. Good-bye! Thank you," and before Jack's mother could say a word the man hurried out.

When Jack ran down to see the train off, he was received with cheers.

"Here," said a man, picking up a train-boy's basket, "let us give them some books and papers—they are always welcome in the country."

"Yes, and so are other things," said a lady who had noticed the poverty of the house, "here is a shawl for Jack's mother."

That started it, and as the basket passed from one car to another, mittens, caps, scarfs, and overshoes were thrown in. Those who had nothing else to spare tied a little money in their handkerchiefs, and threw them in, and, last of all, one man gave an overcoat for Jack. Then the basket was lifted off the train, and put at the boy's feet, and with the passengers crying, "A merry Christmas, Jack!" and, "Three cheers for Jack's mother!" the train went on its way.

—Adapted from a story written in 1891

Lesson 21: Adoration

 STORY

Before your visit with Jesus in the Blessed Sacrament, discuss with your child how adoration is an act of love and how Jesus appreciates every tiny thing we do for love of Him. Read aloud "The Anchoress," starting on the next page.

 PACKET

PAGES 73–82

Compile the Adoration Booklet for bringing to Adoration. Explain that the image on the front cover shows Jesus' willing captivity in the tabernacle, as illustrated in "The Anchoress." Fold pages together and staple. These quiet-time activities can help "draw a child closer to Jesus." If it will not disturb others, let your child bring his booklet and a marker whenever he goes with you to Adoration. Fifteen-minute visits are best at this age.

Draw Close to Jesus

ADORATION

Bring your child to church with you to make a visit to Jesus in the Blessed Sacrament. Your child may want to bring his wrapped "Gifts of Love" from the previous lessons. Encourage your child to ask Jesus to come into his heart and live with him forever. When you leave, your child can bring his "Gifts of Love" home to set on your home altar.

 PACKET

PAGES 67–72

Your child may wish to make a spiritual bouquet (a gift of prayer, good works, or Mass remembrance for the living or dead) as a gift for a friend or family member in need. Your child may choose to spend time in special prayer for the person before the Blessed Sacrament or at home. Afterwards, he can make a spiritual bouquet card for the person, letting him know of the gift offered on his behalf. Unused images from the Mass Book Project or any unused invitations (pages 67–72 in Packet) can be used to make the card. When finished, encourage your child to mail his "I Prayed for You" card.

The Anchoress

The little King was very sad. He sat in the turret of his great gloomy castle and peered over his kingdom, or at least as much of it as he could see. Far away in the distance he could see woods and fields, very small from so far off, like little painted fields and trees, painted blue and green. And then he leaned right out and looked down at the streets that wound around the castle, and at all the twisted chimneys and the gabled houses, and the birds' nests in the gables. He thought, "How friendly the chimneys are, they are always two leaning together; they are never one little one alone."

And he leaned out further still until he could see the boys playing in the street. They looked funny because he saw them from above; their heads looked round and dark, and when they passed right under him he could see the round head and the clogged feet only, no body in between, so that they looked like balls with feet.

"How happy they are," he sighed. "They are not like me, all alone because I am a King."

But he leaned so far out of the window that my Lord Cardinal, who had been watching him all the time, drew him in by the heels. "Your Majesty must be robed for the procession now," he said.

The King stamped his foot; he was weary of processions, weary of kingship. "I will not lead it, my Lord Cardinal; I am tired of being king. Make some other boy king. It is all processions and receptions and lessons. Have done; I will stay here today."

My Lord Cardinal looked gently at him. "Nay, do not strive against God's will. He it is Who has made you king. It is a wearisome thing for a little boy, but we all find God's will for us tedious sometimes." He bent down, smiling, and whispered into the King's ear, "It is a wearisome thing sometimes to be a cardinal; it would often be a great joy to wear the shoes of the old priest in the town, who plays with the boys in the street."

"I will be King no more," raged the boy. "Today I will stay here. I hate my processions." But my Lord Cardinal took his hand and led him to his robing room.

That night the King fell to turning somersaults and was scolded by the royal tutor. "Do you not know," he said, "that you are the Lord's anointed?" And he bore the Lord's anointed, struggling and screaming with temper, to the highest turret of all and locked him in for punishment. This turret was quite empty. It was very seldom used, since the King was seldom punished. But of late his tantrums had become unbearable to the whole court.

The turret was quite empty, or so it seemed at first, and it was growing dark, for there was only a slit for a window; but presently the King heard a twittering in the corner, and there, built right into the wall, was a nest of young birds. The King sat very still and watched them, and presently through the slit came their mother, flying with a crumb of bread in her mouth.

"Where did you get that crumb?" asked the King, for he knew that his people were very poor and scarcely had bread for themselves.

"From the anchoress," said the bird, and although it was dusk she broke into a merry little singing.

"Who is the anchoress?" said the King.

"Oh, well," said the bird, "she is the anchoress,

just the anchoress," and away she flew, into the dusk again.

The next time she came through the slit she bore a golden straw in her beak. "That is for my nest," she sang.

"Who gave you the straw?" asked the King.

"The anchoress," said the bird.

"*Who* is the anchoress?" shouted the King.

The bird put her head on one side and thought. Then she put it on the other side and thought again. Then she hopped round and round, thinking harder still. "Oh dear, oh dear," she twittered, "I've been thinking so hard for the answer that I have forgotten the question!"

"Who is the anchoress?" said the King.

"Oh, yes! the anchoress. That's who she is."

Presently the royal tutor unlocked the door and led the King to his chapel for night prayers. He was not at all pious, but he knelt in his stall with his hands folded on his cushion of red plush and the arms of his family blazoned in gold on the great flag hanging behind him, and he looked very prayerful. He had learned that he must kneel straight and close his eyes, but all the time he was thinking about the little twisty streets winding around the castle. "I don't expect *those* boys have to say their prayers," he thought. But out loud he said, "Amen," and then his page, bearing a long taper, led him to bed.

When the King lay in his silken sheets, his bright hair flowing over the pillow, the door opened softly and my Lord Cardinal crept in. "I have a rosy apple for Your Majesty," he said.

The King sat bolt upright. "Be seated, my Lord," he said, and the old man sat on his bed. "Tell me a story," said the King. "But no, tell me instead, who is the anchoress?"

My Lord Cardinal lifted the King into his arms and carried him to the window. The streets were all dark and the chimneys huddled together against a pale sky. Far away beyond the houses one little light burned, like a single star, in a turret that stood against the church.

"Do you see that light?"

"Yes."

"That is her light. The anchoress is a lady who lives all alone in a turret that has no door, only one little window through which men pass her bread and water. That window looks on the world, on all the poverty and sickness and sin, and on all the riches and foolishness that pass the window. And, inside, another little window looks into the church, on all the treasure and healing and holiness and all the sacrifice and wisdom of Heaven."

"How silly of her to live alone in that turret," said the King. "She could be free and run in the street."

My Lord Cardinal put the King back to bed. "I could not make Your Majesty understand," he said, "not yet. One day it may be that Our Lord Christ will make you wise. Now eat your apple and go to sleep. God bless you, little son."

There was a hue and cry in the castle. During the night the King had vanished! Except for the core of an apple, the royal bed was empty. Pages ran to and fro wringing their hands; heralds went out blowing great blasts on their trumpets in the streets; the ministers gathered together in council; the soldiers stood in a row with their swords in their hands; and no one had any idea of what to do next. The royal wardrobe was examined but none of his suits were missing; the pages were forced to think, with a blush of shame, that the King was somewhere, where they knew not, clothed only in a shirt and his long hose. Further search proved that he was unwashed.

When the King slipped out of the great gate, he ran as fast as his legs could carry him to the other end of the town. When he dared to stop and look around, he found himself in a poor street where the little houses were so old that they were leaning on one another for comfort, and all the doors were crooked. In this street a lot of boys were playing leapfrog. At first the King wondered why they did not bow to him and stop playing; then his heart leaped for joy. "I'm never going to be a king again," he said to himself.

Suddenly the boys saw him and they began to laugh at him. One of them came up and asked him who he was.

"No one," said the King. "Can I play with you?"

"Why have you got no coat?" said a little girl.

The King flushed; he suddenly understood that he looked very odd and that they were all laughing at him. He was beginning to be hungry for his breakfast too. Then from a long way off he heard the sound of the trumpets, and he knew that they were searching for him.

"Please, please hide me!" he cried, but the children ran away.

He knocked, though very timidly, on a door. It opened and a woman let him in.

"Who are you?" she asked.

"I don't know." The King hung his head; he dared not say who he was. The woman had five children and they crowded around him.

"He must be lost," said one.

"He has no coat," said another.

"He doesn't know who he is," said a third.

The fourth could only say "Mama," and the fifth could not say anything.

"Poor thing," said the woman, "he is shivering cold." She looked around for a coat. " 'Tis a pity we have no coal to light a bit of fire for him. Has anyone a coat?"

The eldest boy took off his own and put it on him, and the King's arms stuck out of it at the elbows because it was so worn; but he was glad of its warmth. One of the little girls gave him some

clogs, but they hurt his feet, and the kind woman gave him a piece of black bread and some warm milk. When he had eaten he went into the street with the five children, and they began to play leapfrog; but he stumbled in his heavy clogs and fell whenever he tried to run.

Then suddenly the trumpets blared out again. They were near now. The King stood still and listened. A man ran down the street. "Make way," he shouted, sweeping them all aside with his arms, "make way, the King is lost," and he pushed the King over into the gutter and hurried on, shouting the news. All the doors were flung open, heads shot out of every window, people ran out of the houses. The King was lost among them! But the eyes of the boy whose coat he wore were fixed on him; they traveled from the silken hose to the fine golden hair, and suddenly the boy drew away from him as if he were afraid. The King knew that he had guessed. He turned and ran.

When the sun had gone down, the King crept out from under a low archway, where he had hidden nearly all day, and looked around him. He was stiff and cold and hungry. He found that he had run a long way, to the very outskirts of the town, and looking up he saw that he stood under the turret where the anchoress dwelt. It was a little turret and built not very high. He suddenly thought he would climb up and speak to her; perhaps she would not fear him. He took his clogs off and scrambled up. Her window was crossed with bars and he was able to hold on to them, and pushing his feet into a crevice in the wall he peered in.

The anchoress did not see him. She was a very little lady, clothed like a nun, and she was kneeling with her back turned, looking through the window into the church. And through that window another little King looked back at her. He was very small. A heavy crown of gold was pressing another crown of thorns on his forehead; a great chasuble weighted with jewels was covering his slender little body. He had put his hands through the bars for the anchoress to hold, and she was kissing them because they were wounded.

Then the earthly King heard the other King speak: "Tell me a story," He said, in a child's voice.

The anchoress laughed low and sweetly; her laughter was very tender. "But Your Majesty knows that I know only one, and You have heard it so often.

"I want to hear it again!"

"Oh, my love, how patient You are! Do you want to hear yet again the story of the King's Son Who came disguised as a poor boy to win the heart of a beggar maid, because she would have run away if she had seen Him in his royal splendor?"

"Yes, that one," said the thorn-crowned Boy.

The other little boy listening was astonished. It was the story that was written in all his fairy books and he had heard it over and over again; only now, for the first time, he knew it was true!

At the end of the story, the anchoress turned around and saw the other listener. She smiled at him and the earthly King asked her, "Who is He?" She crossed the room to him, where he was clinging to the window that opened into the world.

"He is the King," she said. "Do you not see His crown? He is the King of Heaven and earth, but no one seems to want Him. He is so much alone. They don't understand His human Heart that longs for other boys to come and be with Him. Sometimes they come, but more often He is left alone, and all the sound of the world's sin and sorrow comes in through the window to Him, all day, all night!"

"Can't He go away?"

"Yes," the anchoress said, "but He will not. You see, He loves them. All the poor silly people are His subjects, so He stays here to be among them; and you know His friends understand, and some of them like me live alone too, so that instead of the sound of sad things, He can sometimes be with His friends and hear lovely stories."

The voice of the anchoress grew faint and sounded far away, like the clear sound of a tiny stream flowing in a rock, and the King suddenly found himself taken by the heels and brought down into the Cardinal's arms. The Cardinal was dressed as an ordinary priest, a black cloak covering him, a broad black hat on his head. The King and the Cardinal looked at each other and laughed.

"All day I sought Your Majesty, and many a boy I played with in the street," said my Lord Cardinal. And then softly, "Was it a great day for *you too,* my dear King?"

Back in the castle, the King clothed again in his royal robes, the Cardinal in his scarlet, the King said, "My Lord Cardinal, tell me that old story."

"Are you not weary of it?"

"No."

The King fell asleep listening, and my Lord Cardinal said to the little bird who perched on the window's ledge with a golden straw in her beak, "We are all in our place, all alone with Our Lord, each of us: you in your nest, I in my scarlet, the King in his robes, the poor boy in the street. If we try to be good, we are all little anchorites telling the story of our life to the King to comfort Him."

—*Adapted from a story by Caryll Houselander*

The church is big, so dim, so still,
Where Jesus stays all day,
I think You must be lonesome, Lord,
I'll slip inside and pray.